Becoming a
Conscious Leader:

Gateway to the Fifth Dimension

Dr. Omar Clark Fisher, M.Ed. MSM, PhD.

To order additional copies of this book, contact:
Xlibris
844-714-8691
www.Xlibris.com
Orders@Xlibris.com

ISBN: Softcover   978-1-6698-4446-4
        EBook   978-1-6698-3599-8

Print information available on the last page

Rev. date: 09/19/2022

Call to Action

Humankind has now entered the cosmic Age of Aquarius. Consequently, we are transiting out of the Age of Information. Many of our collective acquired habits are being controlled by energies and forces which no longer serve us. Age of Aquarius features knowledge, expansion of awareness and mental acuity plus the potential for evolution of human Conscious.

As we cross the threshold and progress into the 3rd decade of the 3rd Millennium, time is ripe now to re-examine and reflect upon mankind's styles of leadership. Most likely, what got us here will be wholly inadequate to empower and uplift humanity beyond mere survival.

The singular most pressing challenge today is nurturing Conscious Leaders – those inspiring and compassionate persons who we can trust, can follow or use as role models.

> "Effective leaders outperform ineffective leaders- every time....business performance is directly tied to effective leadership and the most effective leaders are conscious, authentic leaders." Bill Adams, Leadership Circle Blog 2014

This book is an action-oriented guide to becoming a Conscious Leader. The first section explores in some detail what is Conscious-ness, its history and what science research reveals to us about the workings of the human brain fixated on the 2D/3D reality. The second section reviews what is modern business leadership, common best practices and what is missing in leadership theories that focus on maximizing shareholder ROI. A broader success measure is required to propel us forward. Proposed are 3 key ROIs— return on Investment (capital); return on Inspiration (higher consciousness); and return on Integrity (authenticity).

The third section describes the benefits of Conscious Leaders and suggests a pathway to transform yourself from a great Leader into a Conscious Leader, at the gateway to the 5th Dimension. Conscious Leaders think with their hearts as well as their minds. For mankind to thrive, our collective future depends less about technologies than leadership. Remember our future is all in <u>your</u> hands!

21st CE Symbol for Conscious Balance is a modified Yang-Yin symbol.

One Whole with 4 complementary Elements – opposites interspersed and integrated by Unity that is All & Everything; surrounded with phases of the Moon depicting movement.

Yin and Yang. / (jɪn) / noun. Are **two complementary principles in Chinese philosophy**: Yin is negative, hard, wet, dark, and feminine/ moon, night; Yang positive, bright, soft, warm, dry, and masculine/ sun, daylight. Their interaction is thought to maintain the harmony of the universe and to influence everything within it.

Few ancient philosophies have been as influential as Taoism. Developed in the 4th century B.C., the philosophy is centered around the achievement of 'the Way' and finding harmony and balance within. At the heart of this philosophy is the symbol that has come to represent it as its most identifiable aspect: the Yin and Yang.

Modified here with moon phases, representing transition out of darkness into light.

======================= /

Exercise: Location of Conscious Leader by Conscious Leadership Group

Listen: https://youtu.be/Q5Ofcnr_Z7I

Visit: www.conscious.is

Contents

Acknowledgements

Many colleagues have contributed ideas to this EBook and the concept of Conscious Leaders, too many to name individually here. Suffice to say that this is a work in progress, with more enhancements yet to come. Special thanks is given to Excalibur Institute (Thailand), GoGlobal Business School (Singapore) and Muhammed Lameen Abul-Malik (Dubai).

Your feedback and comments, dear Reader, are most welcome to further embellish and improve this endeavor.

Part 1. Why Write this EBook

Humankind has now entered the cosmic Age of Aquarius. Consequently, we are transiting out of the Age of Information. Collectively, we have acquired habits and are being controlled by energies and forces which no longer serve us. Age of Aquarius features knowledge, expansion of awareness and mental acuity plus the potential for evolution of human Conscious[1]. As we cross the threshold and progress into the 3rd decade of the 3rd Millennium, time is ripe to examine and reflect upon humanity's maturation over the previous 2 thousand years.

What major lessons have we learned? Certainly, humankind shed its primary focus on survival, outgrew hunting and gathering for food and water, leveraged new tools and technologies to develop urban centers, seaports, airports and launched scientific instruments into outer space to probe the dark stars and distant planets. Most recently, the James Webb telescope, replacing the Hubble, is predicted to gather images and gaseous data from light sources dating back to the Big Bang explosive beginning of our Universe. We can measure now accurately to a nano-second. Manmade machines smash atoms and perform 442 Pentaflops of coded instructions per second by supercomputer (Japanese). Nevertheless, the general overall level of human Conscious has failed to keep pace with visible material changes, creature comforts, medical advancements and financial and technological breakthroughs.

Anyone can observe that sustained expressions of mutual tolerance, practice of true compassion, "love than neighbor as thyself" and gratitude for Nature's abundance are presently in very short supply. Even though Conscious Capitalism was first asserted 40

---

1 Throughout the EBook, the author adopts John Dewey's distinction: "Conscious" refers to personal/human state of affairs (i.e. self-reflections) whereas "Consciousness" refers to activities of the Mind like thinking (i.e. self-doings).

years ago, those who willingly practice Conscious Capitalism for their business hardly exceed a handful of companies worldwide.

Hence, this is the perfect time to revisit the "Why" of human creation. Associated questions posed might be: Why are we here? What is the role of humanity on planet Earth at this moment in recorded history? How to advance our emotional intelligence to realize the fullest potential of human beings- including reaching out to embrace the 5th and 6th Dimensions?

My personal journey into Conscious began over 50 years ago and is chronicled in Appendix **A1** to this EBook.

Time is <u>now arrived</u> to evolve beyond abuse and violence towards others who don't look like us, beyond the inhumanity of oppression and deprivation imposed on certain minorities and those in poverty, beyond the senseless hunger and malnutrition foisted upon children and beyond the internecine and cross-border armed conflicts that feeds and sustains profits of weapon manufacturers while slaughtering innocent civilians across the globe annually.

These "old habits" must be over-written with a fresh, invigorating Conscious with a truly humane (moral) compass guiding the human species away from the current path of mutual self-destruction towards a Higher Purpose, world peace and fulfillment of our collective Covenant as Vice-Regent of this Earthly Garden. This is the transition required- and the keystone for such transformation is embodied in Conscious Leaders.

Make no mistake: development of a movement of Conscious Leaders is utmost urgent.

During 2021, at some indeterminant time, mankind transited out of the **Age of Information** (which ostensibly started with the birth of the Darpa Internet 1948), and into the **Age of Conscious**. Concomitantly, we were swept into the Age of Aquarius [commencement between Dec 2020 and March equinox 2021]- which brings to humanity an expanded consciousness, earthly renewal, innovative solutions to lingering social and economic troubles, revitalized cooperation and a summons to higher evolution of our species Conscious towards enlightenment (individual as well as collective).

While there is a marked increase in meditation[2] and the practice of mindfulness is becoming more commonplace – even accepted at many corporate workplaces under burgeoning wellness programs—most probably less than 4.5% of global population is having deliberate and daily focus on their (self) conscious.

Modern research on individual meditators as well on those who meditate in groups at work in corporate settings demonstrate not only significant personal health/well-being benefits, but also heightened productivity at work. Conscious Leaders in business outperform

---

2   Note: meditation here is not a specific method of calming the brain, nor breathing technique, nor yogic posture but rather an act of quiet contemplation or prayer in order to align with one's Higher Self.

conventional leaders in financial benchmarks—including employment satisfaction and returns to stakeholders. Evidence includes:

> "Effective leaders outperform ineffective leaders- every time….business performance is directly tied to effective leadership and the most effective leaders are conscious, authentic leaders." [3]

Referencing the ground-breaking research on corporate performance by CEO John Mackey and Professor Raj Sisodia, Tony Schwartz posited in the Harvard Business Review journal that:

> "Companies that practice Conscious Capitalism perform 10X better."[4]

Therefore, as mankind embarks in a whole new epoch this guidebook intends two (2) inter-related goals:

1. Facilitate an exodus for the vast majority of global population out of the **Age of Information** (Age #4). Just as robots, artificial intelligence and metaverse and enabling digital technologies ensnare and envelop us, we can learn to shift gears so that human imagination and intelligence takes an upper hand. Yet we must be prepared.

   We must unlearn certain "truths" widely accepted and adhered to as conventional wisdom- which in fact are no longer true. Moreover, the global public education system requires a total overhaul as its curriculum teaches rote memorization of obsolete information and behavior patterns and work skills refined in the Industrial Revolution (Age #3); nearly entirely useless in our 21st CE.

2. Describe a framework for understanding the advent of **Age of Conscious** (Age #5), breaking down in some detail what is Conscious and what is Conscious Leadership as the essential baseline mindset, emotional intelligence and human skills required to not simply survive in the **Age of Conscious** but rather to thrive – to carry mankind forward in a fresh invigorating relationship with Mother Earth, with exploration (not conquest) of Outer Space and to become reconciled with our greatest gift – human Conscious – that pure living connection with Divinity and spark of positive co-creation.

---

3   Bill Adams, Leadership Circle Blog, 2014 www.leadershipcircle.com/en/business-results-and-effective-leadership-effective-leaders-outperform-ineffective-leaders-every-time/
4   Tony Schwartz, Harvard Business Review on Corporate Social Responsibility, April 2014.

Part 2. Dilemma

At the end of the 2nd decade of the 21st CE, income inequality and concentration of wealth reached historic proportions- 50% of global population owns 1% of assets whereas 11% controls more than 76% of all financial assets. Some 51 million millionaires own $173 Tril dollars of wealth; this is 1.8 X annual global GDP. In fact, 1% or 79M persons control 38% of global assets valued at $158 Tril (where total global assets are $418.3 Tril[5]).

Top 50 global corporations (MNCs) generate a market capitalization of $24 Tril, which is 2X annual GDP of the bottom 160 countries worldwide, with 35% of global population (2.6 Bil[6]). The Top 10 corporations have accumulated $12.5 Tril in market capitalization – equivalent to the annual GDP of 165 nations with 82% of global population! Staggering amounts of wealth and financial assets have been generated over the past few decades, which testifies to the success of capitalism business model. Yet clearly only a small minority of companies, employees and national economies enjoy these rewards.

Centralization of authority by Central Banks over the past 120 years has resulted in standardization of financial markets, the dominance of fractional banking and explosion of credit (debt). Between the end of WW2 in 1945 and 1972 OPEC oil crisis, the U.S. dollar currency became the de facto global reserve currency—granting unlimited pricing power to the U.S. capitalist economy. Concomitantly, U.S.A. assumed a role of world's policeman empowered by its superpower nuclear military-industrial prowess.

The maturing of the **Age of Information** produced astounding technological advances: space exploration on the surface of Mars, artificial intelligence and robotics facilitating delicate brain surgery and heart replacement, invention of blockchain, smart contracts and instant digitalization of physical assets, and more. However, the price paid by humanity for such technology and financial advances seeking profits at all costs is no less than devastating and, perhaps, irreversible damage in the form of climate over-heating, depletion of rain forests, dislocation of +65 Mil refugees, unchecked hunger and malnutrition or starvation for 690 million people, and recent intermittent pandemics (Spanish Flu, Madcow, AIDS, SARS virus, and CoVid19) which collectively caused approximately 160 Mil deaths.

Violence among mankind is on the rise: 5,226 terrorism incidents[7] afflict on both developed and emerging nations alike from within as hatred and racism, or from outside as religious intolerance and vestiges of colonial oppression.

There is simply no global plan for peace, nor for friendly mutual co-existence.

What is needed now is a **re-set:** before Armageddon due to the push of a button instigating full-on nuclear warhead attacks, or before a death-spiral due to worldwide financial

---

5   Global Wealth Report 2021.

6   Data from United Nations, https://www.worldometers.info/gdp/gdp-by-country (2017).

7   World Terrorism Report 2021, ref. https://www.visionofhumanity.org.

collapse, or before climate change brings an over-heating above 2.0 F degrees (now 1.76 F degrees 2020), making Mother Earth inhospitable to humanity and barren as a sustaining food source.

In reality, there are multiple risks to total elimination of human beings before 2050. Rather than live in constant fear, instead let us **refocus** on the promise of the **Age of Conscious**— to double down on development of Conscious Leaders. Not only to save our planet and our way of Life, but more significantly to nurture the fullest potential of humanity: to cultivate a generation of Conscious Leaders capable to reset capitalism into Conscious Capitalism, to reset corporate organizations into Conscious Businesses and to reset 3D awareness into 5th D and 6th Dimension thinkers who can be the vanguard for 21st CE.

It is important to recognize that Conscious is not a particular "thing" (like a good to be possessed), rather a state of affairs, a Beingness, always evolving, responding to its environment and, with accretion of wisdom (from experience) continuous growth. [8]

Part 3. What is the GAP

Our leaders across business sectors are conditioned since early childhood, educated in B-Schools and persuaded in the corporate workplace to believe that capitalism is the "best" system and financial parameters are the "best" measures of success—both personal and corporate. There is no argument that the previous 300 years of capitalism has generated gigantic advancements to mankind worldwide, a reduction in poverty and assisted with scientific exploration of Outer Space.

How far has business practice progressed beyond Machiavellianism? Recall that pre-16th CE there was no premium on the rental/borrowing of money (i.e. interest) as condemned by church and religious leaders. However, by the 19th and 20th CE fractional banking and manipulation of credit became commonplace, which dramatically impacts the purchasing power of money and the yields to savings of masses of people.

One standout example is the action by USA Federal Reserve Bank that issued $6 Tril more currency within 12 months- equivalent to 24% of America's annual GDP; thereby inflating money supply and devaluing sharply the base currency held by average citizens.

However, leadership that revolves around corporate success, shareholder profits and quarterly earning has failed to eliminate poverty, to eradicate hunger nor to uplift masses of populations through affordable and effective education.

CEO annual pay across the Fortune 500 at $15M is 208X larger than average worker's salary of $72,000 (2021). This is similar across international companies and has risen to

---

8   Hence, the author does not believe that Conscious Leadership is a thing to be achieved. Moreover, he questions whether and how Conscious Leadership is teachable. This EBook is a work in progress to ascertain the answers. Provide us with your feedback at www.consciouswealth.me, or omar@consciouswealth.me email.

all-time heights, where bonuses and stock options among financial institutions especially are distorting risk-sharing in favor of risk-transfer (hedging) that results in massive business failures, bankruptcies and societal disruptions. These outcomes are not due to a lack of laws nor regulations. Rather, such results occur directly due to leaders decisions, incentives and choices.

In truth, Conscious Leadership is about Beingness- a state of being human, fully present, living in the moment with passion, purpose and neutrality. Conscious Leaders are not passive actors, rather fully engaged, active listeners and problem-solvers. Yet Conscious Leaders do not lead from an ego position ("I must be right...") and self-aggrandizement; they are not invested in specific outcomes as much as positive, collective results consistent with higher values and a greater good.

Perhaps an oversimplification- yet Leadership styles (as we shall see onwards) may be divided into two groups[9]:

1. **Conscious Leader** – A leader that is making decisions and is fully aware of how their decisions or behaviors are potentially going to impact others; and
2. **Unconscious Leader** – A leader that makes decisions completely unaware of how their decisions or behaviors are going to impact others. This is because of neglect, selfishness or willing ignorance.

Ms. Farrar-Eagles goes on to match self-awareness of Leaders to the self-awareness of those they lead- company employees, stakeholders and investors. Her view is when the "unaware" lead the equally "unaware", this can only cause "Chaos"; at the very least frustration, conflicts, and manifold lost opportunities.

Diagram #1. Leadership Outcomes Grid

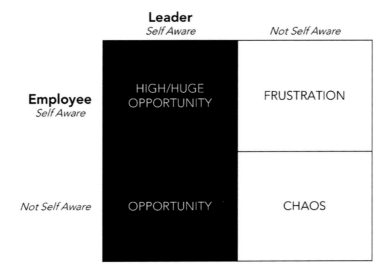

Source: https://www.sunderlandcoaching.com/blog/what-is-conscious-leadership-a-quick-guide

9   Michelle Farrar-Eagles/ Aug. 2020 / https://www.sunderlandcoaching.com

Now, of course, since 2015 corporation managements have increasingly paid attention to ESGs [Environment, Social, Governance] because of scrutiny, compliance or perhaps even conscience, to be nudged into change. Perforce changing corporate outcomes requires first changing Leadership styles—a shift of operating paradigm towards more Conscious Leadership.

In order to better understand what is meant by Conscious Leaders, we intend to separately delve into what is "Conscious" and what is "Leadership". These sections follow.

> **_INSERT EXERCISE 1. – Key Quality Questions to help focus a journey to becoming a Conscious Leader._**

- Q1. What is the Age of Aquarius? Why is this time period important to me?

- Q2. Describe my intention for reading this ebook.

- Q3. If humanity is to evolve its collective consciousness, where might the changes happen? Why are those GAPS significant?

- Q4. How does Conscious influence Leadership in a business context?

- Q5. Is the contemporary inequality of incomes and concentration of wealth in few persons desirable? Are these reversible? If so, how?

Part 4. What is Conscious

It is nearly impossible to capture the pure essence of Conscious in language – rather we typically speak about its mechanisms and influences, i.e. what might be attributes but not Conscious itself. Conscious may be thought of as the Intelligence Force emanating from Source Energy that enlivens and helps order the thousands of Universes expanding across All Creation.

The enlightened Chinese philosopher, Lao Tzu, instructed as much when asked to describe Tao:

"The Tao that can be described is not the enduring and unchanging Tao./ The name that can be named is not the enduring and unchanging name./ (Conceived of as) having no name,/ it is the Originator of heaven and earth; / (conceived of as) having a name,/ it is the Mother of all things." -Lao Tzu Philosopher 6th BCE

"Constantly regard the universe as one living being, having one substance and one soul; and observe how all things have reference to one perception, the perception of this one living being; and how all things act with one movement; and how all things are the cooperating causes of all things that exist; observe too the continuous spinning of the thread and the structure of the web." - Marcus Aurelius (3ʳᵈ CE/AD)

Starting with standard definitions: Consciousness is the awareness of objects and events from the external world and of our own existence and mental processes at any given time. Conscious experience is commonly described as being personal, selective, continuous and changing.

Reported in Webster: Consciousness is: a. the quality or state of being aware especially of something within oneself, and b. the state or fact of being conscious of an external object, state, or fact. Stated previously, "Conscious" is a state of mentality, the recognition of wakefulness.

Despite centuries of dialogue, research, and scientific/technological study there has not emerged a consensus on what precisely is "Human Conscious". It is not the purpose of this EBook to re-examine the myriad of researches, experiments, scholarly books nor philosophical treatises already completed. Rather as author, I intend to present a harmonized viewpoint from my own personal experience that describes a framework for human conscious in support of how **Conscious Leadership** might be teachable.

Harmonization is necessary because the two dominant worldviews on Conscious may be labeled as "Eastern-Mystic" and "Western-Pragmatic" may be understood to be complementary. The former viewpoint concentrates on an inner, spiritual understanding of Conscious as promulgated by Lao Tzu, Buddha, and Maharishi Mahesh Yogi (some examples) whereby an individual strives for a symbiotic and balanced relationship with Nature (Mother Earth) and for claiming a closeness to the Higher Self which may enable enlightenment.

Conversely, the latter viewpoint concentrates on application of brain science, digital technology and experimentation to penetrate the mysteries of the human bio-chemistry and discover the unknowns about mechanisms of Conscious. Since 1950s, many pioneers have added to a collective understanding of how the brain functions (like discovery of human coding of genome)—examples are Dr. Joe DiSpenza and other researchers—nevertheless, origins and composition of Conscious remains a mystery. Partly this is because scientific tools alone are insufficient and handicapped due to human bias and their contamination of the subject matter under investigation.

As we seek to breakout an answer as to "What is Conscious", this author finds Sigmund Freud's 3 tracks a useful starting point to meaningful characterization of Human Conscious:

- (1) Sensations-feelings
- (2) Memory (acting as a pre-conscious reservoir)
- (3) Conscious Perceptions-reason/analysis

Hence, Human Conscious is not simply one Thing- it is an integrated, interactive array of 3 Things.

How might we experience "Conscious"? One interpretation is that silent (serene) gap between moments of Time. A serene "moment" when we are simply breathing automatically in between the seconds as they tick by, or between the more than 80,000 thoughts we think daily. Human Conscious is inseparable from a physical body, as this is the instrument we utilize to confirm Conscious within our Time/Space experience. Yet Conscious exists outside Time/Space as well- its origins are mysterious, infinite and co-existent with its Divine Creator. Commonly, we associate Conscious with Spiritual dimensions, issuing forth similar to an ambassador gushing from the Cosmic Intelligence that orders and breathes Life into all Creation.

Below is a graphic representation of Conscious, using language and images to form a structure[10]

Diagram #2. A Possible Synthesis of Structure to Human Conscious

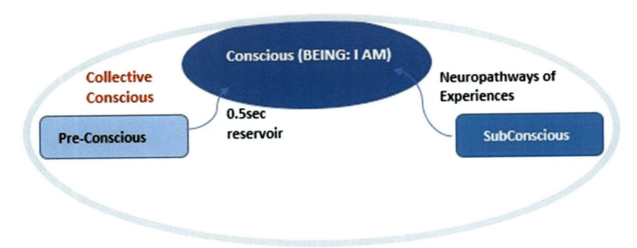

Conscious is my personal experience of BEING: I AM. It is a gateway to the Higher Self integral to the **Collective Conscious**, which participates in Eternal Spirit and Divine Intelligence as sustained by the Divine Creator.

Thus, there are two aspects of Conscious—Inside the Human Body/Mind and Outside.

> INSIDE: My Personal Conscious (also known as Paradigm of Self-Identity and individual Mind)

---

10 Although, pure Conscious is structureless and inter-woven into the cellular fabric of all Things. This Diagram is clearly not definite; it offers a schema to help describe the phenomenon of Conscious from a human perspective.

OUTSIDE: My Conscious flowing into/out of **Collective Conscious**, which is integral to Cosmic Conscious (see Diagram 2) understood as the Prime & Original Creative Intelligence: The Divine Plan for All Creation.

Since Plato, we have accepted the 3 dimensions of space and 1 dimension of time. When applied somewhat differently to the experience of human conscious, it might be described that each person's living participation in 6 dimensions.

Diagram #3. Possible Structure of Cosmic and Human Conscious

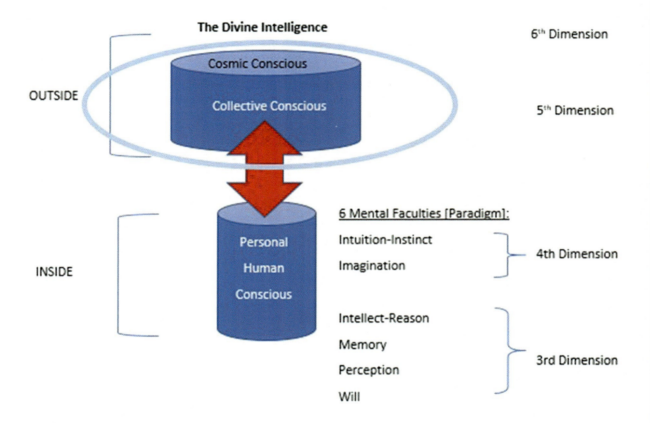

Noteworthy in this Diagram 3. Is the interaction (up/down) between an Individual Conscious and a **Collective Conscious**. Philosophers and scholars have posited, from witnessed personal experiences with heightened Imagination and flashes of Inspiration, that all human knowledge, information and individual experiences are impressed into and accumulated as a **Collective Conscious** ever since the miraculous creation of Adam- the first human being. Recall from Bible and Quran scriptures[11], that Almighty God taught Adam the names of all Things, which silenced and awed the Angels upon his demonstration. We may infer that all the information- in whatever language or as data – ever created co-exists in this Collective Conscious; to which daily is added new information, experiences, and data by the 7.9 billion humans presently living.

---

11   Quran: Version Yusuf Ali translation and Bible: King James version 1948

Individual Conscious-ness is the "fuel" that powers the human car (metaphor) and its vitality. The 6 Mental Faculties are the various integrated features of the physical vehicle (Body) existing in Time/Space. Without this fuel, there is a physical Body as non-living- which eventually disintegrates and dissolves. This Conscious fuel is a high-octane mixture of individual Soul, personal Awareness (that participates in the **Collective Conscious**) and a Divine Spark of Intelligence. Together these shape each unique Person at birth as a gifted Human Being in Time/Space reality. Each **Personal Conscious** can be developed, refined and magnified if deliberately nurtured or, alternatively, can weaken, wither and dissipate if neglected during its lifetime. **Personal Conscious** does not reside solely in the Brain (although your awareness of Being as Consciousness is partly active there); rather **Personal Conscious** moves as Intelligence through every one of the trillions of human cells- giving Life and purpose on the molecular level.

So how to activate, enhance and develop the **Inside** (Personal) **Conscious**?

No one has seen or measured the reaches of the human Mind nor its fuel-Conscious-ness. Hence, there is much dispute and disagreement even among scientific researchers. Until today, we only have images or symbols to describe these. Dr. Thurman Fleet, in 1950, developed an image of the human Mind, which was popularized by Bob Proctor over the past 40 years. The image looks like this:

Diagram #4. Model of Mind-Body

Source: Bob Proctor lecture using model originated by Dr. Thurman Fleet, 1934, USA

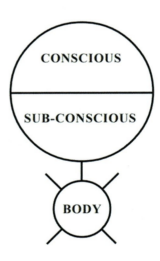

However, this image only accounts for 3 of the 6 Mental Faculties yet still has utility to explain the concept of Paradigm. A Paradigm is a set of habitual patterns in the Brain or neuro-pathways established in the Brain that controls human Thinking, Decisions, Behaviors and Actions—that in turn determine our Results. Conscious Being is the fuel for the car where the speed, direction, distance travelled, comfort or not, efficiency, discipline and more are actually determined by the make-up of the vehicle itself. Core Beliefs and personal Attitude are critical factors in the car's construction, maintenance and performance. Behaviors and habits are learned over time and thus can be unlearned or modified with careful and deliberate goal-setting and adaptation. In short, the neuro-pathways can be re-wired; the car can be repaired, re-tooled or upgraded as necessary.

(This model of the mind and body was originated by the late Dr. Thurman Fleet of San Antonio, Texas in 1934 (circa). Dr. Fleet was the founder of Concept Therapy.)

The fuel, Conscious-ness, on the other hand flows naturally, automatically and purposefully – from an unknown Source Energy carrying within it an unknown Intelligence.

Experimentation until today cannot calibrate Conscious-ness nor inform how to deepen or intensify it. However, a individual can influence this cosmic fuel by:

- Nurturing Self-Awareness
- Developing Mindfulness
- Deepening Spiritual practice
- Alignment with Faith

Two important driving elements in this cosmic fuel are:

- Creativity
- Self-Control

It is imperative that a person deliberately cultivate these 2 elements in themselves in order to deepen and enrich **Inside Conscious**. Why?

Because:

1. **Creativity** is the Core Essence of the Creator and Intelligence that sweeps through the Universe. Human beings are only one (1) unique species of creation- in fact far outnumbered by insects, for example. By nurturing one's innate Creativity, a person aligns with this miraculous and primordial element, which thus deepens and intensifies Self-Awareness (principal component of Conscious in Human Beings). Unfortunately, the public education systems globally demand conformity, rote memorization of curriculum as learning (rather than problem-solving) and "fitting in" through grades and in-school disciplines; hence, eventually, personal creativity is schooled out or minimized as a talent.

2. **Self-Control** – also known as Emotional Intelligence – is crucial to a person's ability to temper lower vibrational emotions (like anger, intolerance, depression) in favor of higher vibrational emotions (such as acceptance, reason, love, joy; see Hawkins' Scale Appendix **A3**). Moreover, Self-control enables challenging Goal-setting – which allows the possibility of willingly changing fundamental behaviors and one's Paradigm. Sustained Self-control yields Self-confidence.

When combined, allowing both Creativity and practiced Self-control to be in the "driver's seat" in the car metaphor that person adapts to a Growth Mindset and an expanding positive Conscious. One can experience this high octane blend- commonly referred to as FLOW STATE. Flow State of Mind also engages the Body is a harmonious manner that we experience as pleasurable, mentally invigorating and advancing us towards a desired (and clearly envisioned) End Goal.

The connection between the imagined End Goal and realizing Flow State is critical – as explained in recent study[12] by Yale University's psychologist's Paul Stillman, Ryan Carlson (management) and David Melnikoff (mathematician).

> "The principles underlying Flow may be unconscious yet they are not random- and work within a biological system that can be described in mathematical terms." These researchers postulate a formula: "The more informative a means is, the more is the flow someone will experience while performing it."

Thus, in summary, the greater the clarity and information surrounding an End Goal, the greater the Flow State and the more likely that Conscious-ness will advance to realize the personal performance necessary to accomplish that End Goal.

What are the Main Attributes of Conscious?

It must be acknowledged first that to define, describe or capture the essence of Conscious is impossible with words—similar to the statement by Lao Tzu about Tao: "The Tao that can be described is not the enduring and unchanging Tao."

However, to advance our understanding here are likely characteristics embedded in Conscious[13]:

- Organizing first principle of the Universe – touches All Things (synonym for Love)
- Issues perpetually from the pure Essence of Divinity – Creator of All there Is
- Autonomous – truly authentic
- Possesses Authority – accepts 100% responsibility, brooks no contradictions
- Intelligence – pure, natural organic purposeful, adhering to an Eternal Plan
- Expanding – self-motivating, evolving, accretive, growth without measure
- Infinite & Eternal Creativity – boundless, beyond Time/Space, totally free
- Living Awareness – awakened, self-renewing, exemplary excellence in both Living Things and Non-Living Things

---

12 Yale Researchers have Formula Getting in the Flow, article by Bill Hathaway, Yale University, May 2022.
13 To know a bit about its Essence by reflecting on its impacts.

Q1. What is a standard understanding and/or definition for "Conscious"?

Q2. When do you feel most "Conscious"? What words might help describe those feelings?

Q3. How many main aspects of Conscious exist? In which ways do these differ?

Q4. Describe the purpose of the "Collective Conscious"?

Q5. Humans live in 3 or 4 dimensions yet posses potential for experiencing a 5th dimension. Comment.

Part 5. Brief History: the Study of Conscious

For thousands of years, philosophers, scientists, mathematicians and inventors have speculated on the nature of Conscious. There are too many opinions to review here. A few highlights can enrich our understanding consistent with the goals of this EBook.

4th CE BC / Plato: used the term "World Soul" to describe the unknowable Conscious Universe. "Thinking: the talking of the soul with itself." Thinking is affirmation of the Self, separately existing and empowered by and capable to Self-Reflection (a state of Conscious-ness).

The Greek thinker Aristotle devised a foundation for psychology in 3rd BCE. He stated that human perception has two dimensions[14]: i) a mental state wherein consciousness is intrinsic, or a higher order of thought informed by forces outside the body, and secondly ii) a qualitative phenomenal nature of an experience itself. Aristotle argues that both dimensions are possible and mutually exclusive because the essence of conscious is (self) reflexive. Unique to the human condition is the Mind's capacity to be self-aware and to communicate in language and images what is perceived.

Rene Descartes, French philosopher, mathematician and scientist in the 17th CE introduced the concept of Mind-Body duality, as being separate subjects yet highly integrated in operation. By 19th CE, the study of the human Mind evolved into a discrete segment of science called psychology.

---

14 Aristotle writings on The Soul, section 3.2 quoted in "Aristotle on Consciousness", by Victor Caston, Oxford Academy Mind Association Journal, Oct 2002, https://academic.oup.com/mind/issue/111/444

"Using a process known as introspection, researchers analyzed and recorded their conscious sensations, thoughts and experiences. They were carefully examining the contents of their own minds."[15]

Psychoanalyst Sigmund Freud identified and described the importance of Conscious and Unconscious functions of the Mind in 19th CE until his passing in 1939 (20th CE).

What are Freud's Three Levels of Consciousness?

In psychoanalytic theory, the three levels of consciousness as outlined by Sigmund Freud are the **conscious, preconscious and unconscious minds.** Freud likened this theory to an iceberg with a visible tip, the conscious mind; an obscured but visible middle, the preconscious; and a bulk hidden beneath the water, the unconscious.

In Freud's model of the mind, the Conscious Mind is formed by the thoughts and feelings that a person is actively aware of and able to reason about. The preconscious is made up of all available memory that has not been accessed by the conscious mind. The unconscious mind consists of repressed instincts, feelings and urges that are negative or shameful. Freud theorized that the preconscious and unconscious exert a powerful influence over the conscious mind without a person's awareness.

Unconscious feelings, thoughts and habits exist in a person as memories, images (usually painful) from the past and are stored as patterns in neuropathways of the brain.

One deep thinker and psychologist is Swiss Carl Jung who explored **Consciousness** from 1900 until 1961.

"Our consciousness does not create itself- it wells up from unknown depths. In childhood it awakens gradually, and all through life it wakes each morning out of the depths of sleep from an unconscious condition."

"Besides a majority of mere recollections, really new thoughts and creative ideas can appear which have never been conscious before."

"The world comes into being when man discovers it. But he only discovers it when he sacrifices his containment in the primal mother, the original state of unconsciousness."

Carl Jung was fascinated with the origins for **Conscious**, which he termed "the collective unconscious" whereby all humans (ever born) are connected to each other and to a shared set of experiences- which could be tapped using primal archetypes: universal symbols for essential aspects of on-going creation; namely, The Great Mother, the Wise Old Man, the Shadow, the Tower, Water, and the Tree of Life. These symbols formed a language with which to communicate inner experiences from past experiences to the Mind because the human brain stores such experiences largely in intense emotional moments as images.

---

15 Wilhelm Wundt first studied internal perceptions (1873) seeking to identify components of human consciousness, which evolved into science of psychology. www.lumenlearning.com.

"If one reflects upon what consciousness really is, one is deeply impressed by the extremely wonderful fact that an event which occurs outside in the cosmos produces simultaneously an inner image. Thus, it occurs within; in other words it becomes conscious."

Carl Jung believed that a primitive person is not a "thinker", he cannot "assert what he thinks" but rather it is something "thinks in him." "The spontaneity of the act of thinking does not lie, casually in his conscious mind, rather in his unconscious."

Only by becoming more Self-Aware can an individual grasp the subtle vibrations of the Higher Self, assume more control over and guidance to his thinking process. Jung asserts that the mysterious, unknowable "unconscious" part of human mind is in control of the thinking process – whether actively when seeking to grasp meaning from practical, empirical experience or more subtly by impressing unconscious archetypes upon the psyche while perceiving that experience in the first instance.

"It is not the world as we know it that speaks out of his unconscious, but the unknown world of the psyche, of which we know that it mirrors out empirical world only in part, and that, for the other part, it molds this empirical world in accordance with its own psychic assumptions. The archetype does not proceed from physical facts but describes how the psyche experiences the physical fact, and in so doing the psyche often behaves so autocratically that it denies tangible reality...."[16]

French astronomer Camille Flammarion put it more concisely when he wrote: "Matter, force, life, thought, are all one ... In reality, there is only one principle in the universe ... embracing all that is and all that possibly can be. That which we call matter is only a form of motion. At the basis of all is force, dynamism, and universal mind, or spirit."

Eloquent insight is provided by Fredrich Schiller, 18th CE in his statement:

"The universe is a thought of God. After this ideal thought-fabric passed out into reality, and the new-born world fulfilled the plan of its Creator—permit me to use this human simile—the first duty of all thinking beings has been to retrace the original design in this great reality; to find the principle in the mechanism, the unity in the compound, the law in the phenomenon, and to pass back from the structure to its primitive foundation. Accordingly to me there is only one appearance in nature—the thinking Being." Fredrich Schiller

One of the great contributors to Quantum Field theory, Erwin Schrodinger, wrote in mid-19th CE:

"Consciousness cannot be accounted for in physical terms. For consciousness is absolutely fundamental. It cannot be accounted for in terms of anything else."[17]

---

16 Collective Works of C.G. Jung, reference on https://carljungdepthpsychologysite.blog
17 As quoted in *The Observer* (11 January 1931); also in Psychic Research (1931), Vol. 25, p. 91.

Freeman Dyson, a prominent physicist, wrote the book, <u>Disturbing The Universe</u>, Harper & Row (1979) in which he applies laws of physics to observe the likely existence of a 5th Dimension[18]- what he labeled as the "third level of mind":

> "It is reasonable to believe in the existence of a third level of mind, a mental component of the universe. If we believe in this … and call it God, then we can say that we are small pieces of God's mental apparatus."

With some conviction, he went on to state: 'I do not think our consciousness is just a passive epiphenomenon carried along by the chemical elements in our brains, but is an active agent forcing the molecular complexes to make choices between one quantum state and another. In other words, *mind is already inherent in every electron* [subatomic particle]."

Gradually, these subjective studies prompted more rigorous and probing investigations into conscious-ness, aided by medical technology advancements. After invention of MRI and other brain-scanning and imaging technologies in 1950s, such as functional magnetic resonance imaging (fMRI) and electroencephalography (EEG), brain research surged into the 1990s.

The neuroscience of Human Conscious advanced remarkably as the habits of the Brain and biology of the Body were studied and documented enabling powerful new insights yet revolving around the consequential affects of changing levels of **Conscious** (i.e. how the brain processes information and images) rather than probing its origins.

Diagram #5. Illustration of MRI imaging of brain activity

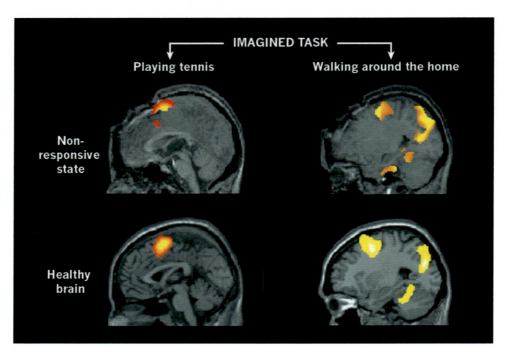

---

18 The author takes poetic license to make this connection of 3rd level with 5th Dimension to gain more clarity.

The yellow colored portions of the MRI images revealed which regions of the brain are activated in response to commands or presentation of images. To a certain degree, these tools have permitted the mapping of physical regions of the human brain and an association to states of alertness.

Whereas studies affirm that brain regions identified as the cerebral cortex and thalamus are important for consciousness. Moreover, activation of the amygdala (mid-brain near hypothalamus region) occurs at times of personal threat, anxiety or rising of fears. Some studies seem to conclude that "unconscious" fears, instinctual and intense emotional responses stimulate the amygdala.

Dr. Peter T. Wallings points out in his illuminating recap of valuable insights[19] contributed by scientists and thinkers over the recent centuries that Dr. Wilder Penfield performed many neurosurgical procedures on patients who were awake in the 1950s. "Thus, he was able to extensively chart the motor and sensory cortex. He concluded that although stimulation of cortical areas may elicit movement or sensation, an intact thalamus and midbrain were also required if conscious awareness or conscious willed action were to occur. If the upper brain stem is the engine of consciousness, the cortex gives us something to be conscious *of*." His observations point to a network effect of Conscious.

Fresh evidence has highlighted a posterior-cortical 'hot zone' that is responsible for sensory experiences.

> "For example, in a 2017 sleep study, researchers roused people throughout the night while monitoring them with EEG.[20] Around 30% of the time, participants who were jolted from sleep reported not experiencing anything just before they woke up. The study showed that those people without conscious experiences during sleep had lots of low-frequency activity in the posterior-cortical region of their brains before waking. People who reported that they had been dreaming, however, had less low-frequency activity and more high-frequency activity."

A confluence of experiments seems to point to an observation that **Conscious-ness** is not confined to one region of the human brain- rather multiple regions are inter-related as neural pathways, chemical transmitters and select cellular zones are simultaneously engaged.

Pioneering physicist Sir James Jeans wrote: "The stream of knowledge is heading toward a non-mechanical reality; the universe begins to look more like a great thought than like

---

19 Source: Dr. Wallings, "Conscious: a brief review of the riddle", Baylor University Medical School, 2000, USA.
20 Nature magazine, "Decoding the neuroscience of consciousness" Sam Falconer, article printed in *Nature* **571**, S2-S5 (24 July 2019); https://www.nature.com/articles/d41586-019-02207-1#ref-CR4

a great machine. Mind no longer appears to be an accidental intruder into the realm of matter, we ought rather hail it as the creator and governor of the realm of matter."[21]

One possible conclusion by scientific inquiry is that our Universe is **energy**- wave and **matter**-particle as well as simultaneously a **mental and spiritual construct**. It may be deduced that **Conscious** is The Prime organizing, force and intelligence that appears to us to be sentient.

Levels of Conscious-ness

Can a person be sensing **Conscious** without an awareness of Time? If **Conscious** is the gap between moments of Time, then pure **Conscious** can be imagined as participation in the Divine flow of Eternal Intelligence, and hence must be Timeless. Humans cannot have a "memory" of the mental condition of such a Timeless state of affairs. There certainly can be recall of the pre-cursor —that temporary state of mind just prior to Mindfulness (a kind of emptiness occurring with non-thinking) – and recall of an exit point– the re-opening of eyes, sensations of returning to a physical, pulsating Body; yet the moments of pure **Conscious-ness** are not "measurable" by us, nor captured by Time/Space parameters.

Are there different states of consciousness?

Modern science has studied various states of Consciousness, which have measurably differing levels of Conscious awareness and experience-- often associated with different patterns of activity. Commonly, these are: wakefulness, daydreaming, REM sleep, and deep sleep. Other less common Conscious states have health and medical diagnosis; including anesthesia, coma, vegetative state, and unresponsive wakefulness. For simplicity, these are outside the scope of this EBook.

Some researchers have suggested that there are up to 7 Levels of Consciousness. Vedic Philosophy labels these 7 levels, that can be associated with human behaviors as exhibited and the dominant feelings a person experiences in reaction to his/her real world.

Level 1 - The Victim
Level 2 - The Emotional Self
Level 3 - The Authentic Self
Level 4 - The Loving Self
Level 5 - The Truthful Self
Level 6 - The Knowing Self
Level 7 - Higher Self Awareness

Source: www.barrettacademy.com

However, consistent with the theme and analysis of this EBook of keeping things simple, Conscious can be said to exist on 3 levels [ref. Part 4, p.11] as displayed below:

---

21 R.C. Henry, "The Mental Universe", NATURE, Vol. 436, July 2005.

A. Individual Human Conscious Experience

This level integrates 4 aspects:

Mental activity– active awareness, wakefulness, sleep, memories, subconscious (patterns, habits) which form a paradigm

Biological activity – heart coherence, the body's autonomic system (breathing, immunity), muscle memories

Cellular presence – home of true Self-Identity, DNA, lineage & legacy

Spiritual presence– an Individual Soul and its connection to infinite Ever-Soul

B. Collective Conscious

Participation with a Higher Self, includes Imagination, inspiration and connection to the totality of and unbroken link to Collective Conscious [ref. Diagram #2 p. 11]

C. Cosmic/Universal Conscious

The Ever-Soul or Divine Intelligence [truly unknowable]; Cosmic Spiritual Essence; link to Divine Spark and Origins of Creation plus on-going as Universal Infinite Intelligence with a Plan. All there is within and outside Time/Space.

Human Beings have a knowing experience of **Conscious** as these 3 Levels inter-twined, as one state of affairs like a "river" fed by 3 streams (or astral planes).

Popular Posited Theories of Conscious-ness

As stated earlier, despite the manifold studies of consciousness there is yet no universally accepted consensus definition. Descartes proposed the idea of *cogito ergo sum* ("I think, therefore I am"), which suggested that the very act of thinking demonstrates the reality of one's existence and consciousness. This idea correlated thinking with consciousness. Today, consciousness is generally equated with awareness of oneself (Inside) and the world (Outside), but debates proliferate on what is the true nature of "awareness", its origins and how it flows into and throughout the Body/Mind.

Modern research on consciousness focuses on the neuroscience behind human conscious experiences: "Scientists have even utilized brain-scanning technology to seek out specific neurons that might be linked to different conscious events."[22]

---

22 IBID, R.C. Henry.

Two major theories of consciousness have emerged[23]: integrated information theory and global workspace theory.

Integrated Information Theory

This approach looks at consciousness by learning more about the physical processes that underlie our conscious experiences. The theory attempts to create a measure of the integrated information that forms consciousness. The quality of an organism's consciousness is represented by the level of integration.

This theory tends to focus on whether something is conscious and measures to what degree it is conscious against a mandated scale.

Global Workspace Theory

This theory suggests there is a memory bank from which the brain draws information to form the experience of conscious awareness. While Integrated Information Theory focuses more on identifying whether an organism is conscious, the Global Workspace Theory offers a much broader approach to understanding how conscious-ness works.

Neither theory, however, is effective in explaining the origins of Conscious, its "substance", how it influences the human Body/Mind, nor how human Conscious might be enhanced or intensified.

Hints How to Enhance Self-Conscious

To date there are only glimpses by science into Conscious. Hence, steps how to enhance Self-Conscious(ness) are truthfully only informed speculation. Yet we can benefit from such musings.

> "Men do not attract that which they want, but <u>that which they are</u>. The "divinity that shapes our ends" is in ourselves; it is our very Self. Only himself manacles man: thought and action are the gaolers of Fate—they imprison, being base; they are also the angels of Freedom—they liberate, being noble. Not what he wishes and prays for does a man get, but what he justly earns. Circumstances, however, are so complicated, thought is so deeply rooted, and the conditions of happiness vary so, vastly with individuals, that a man's entire soul-condition (although it may be known to himself) cannot be judged by another from the external aspect of his life alone." – James Allen, <u>As a Man Thinketh</u>, 1902

> "All experience is in its degree conscious. . . .We must ascribe consciousness to every living agent, such as a plant cell or bacterium, and even (if the

---

23 www.Researchgate.net, article in Brain and Neurosciences Advances Journal, Anril K. Seth, "Conscious the last 50 Years", Feb 2018.

continuity of nature is not to be broken) to an electron." – W. E. Agar Philosophy of organisms, 1948[24]

Tapping into insights from the German philosopher Georg Wilhelm Friedrich **Hegel** (18th into 19th CE):

> "The goal to be reached is the mind's insight into what knowing is. Impatience asks for the impossible, wants to reach the goal without the means of getting there. The length of the journey has to be borne with, for every moment is necessary, … because by nothing less could that all-pervading mind ever manage to become conscious of what itself is — for that reason, the individual mind, in the nature of the case, cannot expect by less toil to grasp what its own substance contains." – Hegel

American Richard Conn Henry, Professor of Physics and Astronomy, John Hopkins University (born 1940-) once said: 'One benefit of switching humanity to a correct perception of the world is the resulting joy of discovering the mental nature of the Universe."

Hence, an individual's mental activity – his/her thinking and giving meaning to sensations – participates in the World Soul (Plato's term similar to *the Collective Conscious*) and impacts its very existence in real time as well as marks it for infinity with "indelible ink."

Part 6. Science of Conscious in the Body

"Looking for consciousness in the brain is like looking in the radio for the announcer." – Nassim Haramein, physicist (born 1961-)

Neuroscientists believe that, in humans and mammals, **the cerebral cortex** is the "seat of consciousness," while the midbrain reticular formation and certain thalamic nuclei may provide gating and other necessary functions of the cortex.[25]

In the past, conscious-ness was thought to emanate from the frontal hemispheres of the brain, but current research has found that the content of consciousness **mainly originates from the hindbrain**[26], as integral with observations of neuro-networks across the brain.

The cerebrum is the largest brain structure and part of the forebrain (or prosencephalon). Its prominent outer portion, **the cerebral cortex**, not only processes sensory and motor information but enables consciousness, a person's ability to consider Self as well as their perceived outside world.

---

24 W.E. Agar, "The Wholeness of the Living Organism", Journal of the Philosophy of Science Vol 15, July 1948 as quoted in JSTOR.org, online library.
25 "Consciousness: a brief review of the riddle", article by **Peter T. Walling, MD**
26 Consciousness: New Concepts and Neural Networks – NCBI. https://www.ncbi.nlm.nih.gov

What maintains consciousness in the brain?

The brain stem connects the cerebrum with the spinal cord. It contains a system of nerve cells and fibers (called the reticular activating system) located deep within the upper part of the brain stem. This system controls levels of consciousness and alertness.

"Consciousness is often described as the mind's subjective experience. Whereas a basic robot can <u>unconsciously</u> detect conditions such as color, temperature or sound (using programmable artificial intelligence coding), <u>consciousness</u> describes the qualitative feelings that are associated with those perceptions, together with the deeper processes of reflection, communication and thought" says Matthias Michel, a philosopher of science and a PhD student at Sorbonne University in Paris.

Does the human heart have consciousness?

Steven Novella explains, "Neurons alone do not equal mind or consciousness. It takes the specialized organization of neurons in the brain to produce cognitive processes that we experience as the mind." So despite the presence of neurons in the heart, we can see that **the heart does not have a mind of its own**. However, recent medical findings by Dr. J. Andrew Armour (in 1991), while studying heartbeats discovered that the heart has a "little brain", or an "intrinsic cardiac nervous system." This "heart-brain" is composed of approximately 40,000 neurons that are like neurons in the brain, meaning that **the heart has its own nervous system** but not a brain.

Does the heart actually think?

Despite not having an "independent brain", the human heart, in addition to its other functions, actually possesses heart-brain coherence composed from the 40,000 neurons that can sense, feel, learn and remember. This heart-brain sends messages to the head-brain about how the body feels and more. This information is crucial for the head-brain to signal and sustain overall well-being of the body.

Does the heart have conscious intelligence?

Researchers noted above reveal the heart to be a command center of formidable intelligence and intuitive knowledge that is tied into every system and every cell of our body. One of the key discoveries is the human heart contains its own independent nervous system: we recognize when the heart "feels" strong emotions (remember that emotion is Energy in Motion). Pioneering research was done by heart surgeon Dr. Reinhard Friedl who captures the findings with living humans using a heartbeat counter. He recognizes that vibrations within the body resonant differently in the heart: **"Good "heartbeat counters" feel and can measure emotions such as fear and anger (but also joy) considerably more intensely than those who were less well able to feel their heartbeat."**[27]

---

27 Dr. Reinhard Friedl, The Source of All Things: A Heart Surgeon's Quest to Understand Our Most Mysterious Organ, St. Martin's Press, NY USA, 2021.

Such observations give further credence to Dr. Hawkins' Map of Consciousness (2012) described in Appendix A3.

Diagram #6 displays the heart-brain areas with keen attention to location of the sensitive nerve ganglia identified in yellow:

Diagram #6. Heart-Brain

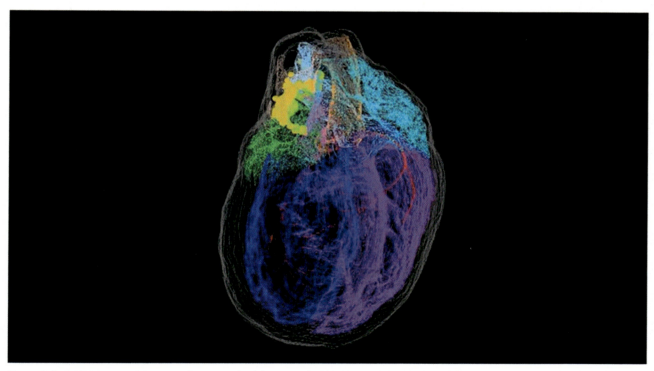

SCIENCE VISUALIZED   NEUROSCIENCE

A new 3-D map illuminates the 'little brain' within the heart

Nerve cells in the organ are poorly understood

Nerve cells (yellow) that make up a heart's "brain" cluster around the top of this reconstructed rat heart, near where blood vessels enter and exit the organ. Other colors show the contours of distinct heart areas, such as the left atrium (green), right atrium (teal), left ventricle (blue) and right ventricle (purple).

S. ACHANTA ET AL//SCIENCE 2020

Source: A new 3-D map illuminates the 'little brain' within the heart, at https://www.sciencenews.org

At this point we have explored What and How is Conscious, a brief history of Consciousness scientific inquiry, and where in the Body might Conscious-ness be located. Thus, it is now appropriate to shift to the topic of Leadership. The narrative first reviews traditional Leadership in order to establish a basis for comparison to Conscious Leadership.

Q1. How many parts to human Conscious as per Sigmund Freud and the functions of each?

Q2. Which parts of the brain participate in Conscious? Using MRI imaging technology, what does modern science tells us about states of consciousness?

Q3. "Conscious" is said to exist on 3 levels. What are each of these and how do they differ?

Q4. Bodily Conscious is experienced separately by the brain and the heart. Describe how these are distinct and how these work cooperatively.

Part 7. What is Leadership

Just as unique as Conscious Intelligence is to human species, is the capacity for Leadership. While mammals and other animals move in "schools" or similar groupings, there is no evidence that a leader is methodically educated or trained in these groups to behave in distinctive ways.

Next, we ask "What is Leadership?"

Peter Drucker, the dean of achieving excellence in management in the 20th CE, defined leadership as: **"Leadership is the lifting of a man's vision to higher sights, the raising of a man's performance to a higher standard, the building of a man's personality beyond its normal limitations."**

One description in the Harvard Business Review states:

"Leadership is the accomplishment of a goal through the direction of human assistants. A person who successfully marshals human collaborators to achieve particular ends is a leader."

Leadership arises due to the confluence of vision, a persuasive personality and superior performance. The commonly understood context for American Drucker, and his followers, is a corporation (or business) competing within a capitalist system. Being clear on this context is crucial to a proper understanding of 20th CE Leadership ("Traditional Leadership") because comparisons to Drucker's perceived "normal limitations" involve measurement of corporate/enterprise performance- largely measured by financial benchmarks. Namely: balance sheet, income and cashflow statements, ROE and ROI, share price, etc.

While there is no definitive set of traits for successful business leaders, these traits appear as most prominent:

Table #1. Top 9 Qualities of a Great Leader

- **Vision.** ... has purpose, passion, inspiration
- **Strategic & Critical Thinking.** ... Values, strategy and analysis
- **Solution-Oriented**...innovative, growth mindset, flexible
- Interpersonal **Communication.** ... builds teamwork, sustainability& collaboration
- **Authenticity & Self-Awareness.** ... astute Self-awareness, personal clarity, integrity
- **Persistence**... a blend of resourcefulness, courage, patience
- **Open-Minded** & Creative. ... emotional intelligence, resilient, & imaginative
- **Motivates** & Rewards Performance– gives direction, delegates, displays service & caring
- **Responsibility**...takes full responsibility for decisions & choices, is dependable, reliable

Moreover, Traditional Leadership evidences four (4) distinct types of styles or behaviors: **Directive, Supportive, Participative, and Achievement-oriented**. As described by House and Mitchell (1974)[28] each leadership style is appropriate for a different business situation when pursuing a path-to-goal approach. Leadership behaviors are adaptive to environment and employee attitudes. A Leader's 3 primary objectives are: i) clarify the path to the goal, ii) helps remove roadblocks, and iii) shapes rewards along the path.

These are summarized as:

Table #2.

Leadership Style	Pattern of Subordinate	Environment	Comments
Directive	Seeks authority leadership; external locus of control; low ability	Complex or ambiguous tasks; strong formal authority structure; good working group	Task-oriented
Supportive	Does not want authority leadership; internal locus of control; high ability	Simple or serial tasks; weak formal authority; No good working group	Employer-oriented

---

28 House, R. J., & Mitchell, T. R. (1997). Path-goal theory of leadership. In R. P. Vecchio (Ed.), *Leadership: Understanding the dynamics of power and influence in organizations* (pp. 259–273). University of Notre Dame Press

Participative	Wants involvement; internal locus of control; high ability	Complex or ambiguous tasks; either strong/weak formal authority; either good or no good working group	Employee-oriented
Achievement-oriented	Seeks authority Leadership; external locus of control; high ability	Simple or serial tasks; strong formal authority; either good or no good working group	Goal/ Achievement-oriented
Source: www. bealeader.net/.org			

Then what makes for good leadership? In short, a role model business leader creates and nurtures other leaders.

This is done because a good leader **possesses a clear vision, is courageous, has integrity, honesty plus humility, clear focus and can motivate others**. Importantly, Drucker emphasized that "management is getting things done through people." Hence, a leader must be a believer in teamwork as well as envision the "Big Picture" as a strategic planner.

When observing effective business leadership in action, Drucker stated[29] that the difference between success and failure in an organization is its leaders. Moreover, he urged continuous learning upon business leaders as well as the necessity to nurture future leaders. To summarize:

1. The essence of leadership is very simple. It is to help people to perform to their maximum potential to achieve organizational goals or objectives.
2. One person can make the difference between success or failure in any organization. You can be that person through becoming a leader.
3. Most people become successful only through the help of others. You can obtain this help through the practice of leadership.
4. You don't need to be a manager to be a leader. You don't need to wait to be promoted. You can become a leader immediately by raising your hand and volunteering to lead.
5. Good leadership doesn't depend on good deals or pleasant working conditions. Your ability to motivate people to perform to their maximum is independent of these factors.

The accepted methods of identifying and measuring good leadership in business typically is in reference to financial performance (mostly quantitative factors- which are more easily calibrated than quantitative measures). Thus, attention is given to outcomes desired in

29 Peter Drucker as referenced in www.corporatelearningnetwork.com

job descriptions, corporate KPIs like topline revenue or earnings growth, ROE and ROI to Shareholders, etc.

INSERT EXERCISE 4. – Key Quality Questions to help focus a journey to becoming a Conscious Leader.

Q1. What is the common understanding of Leadership in a business context?

Q2. Name the top 6+ qualities of a good Leader.

Q3. There are 4 main styles of Leadership. What are the main features of each and which circumstances accords best with each style?

Q4. Are Leaders born or trained? Why do you believe so?

Q5. Which are the main metrics for measuring good Leaders?

Chris Colbert's Highly Transformational Habits

Chris Colbert, former Managing Director of Innovation Lab at Harvard University, states there are 7 Habits of Highly Transformative Leaders[30] . As a keen observer of swift, digital-technology driven change to corporate organizations, he affirms that business leaders today must evolve and adapt to a new set of behaviors if the leaders themselves want to feel fulfilled as well as lead their business enterprises to sustained success.

Rapid change brings conflict and stress happening across a workforce to the surface as most people prefer their own "comfort zone" and tend to resist change. Across the modern capitalist economy, 57% of all employees "report a negative work environment"[31] and nearly 2/3 of workers express discontent and feel isolated, disinterested at their workplace. No wonder there is rampant dissatisfaction, stress and loss of productivity associated with modern work. Change begins with leadership.

Habit #2 of transformative leaders is creating psychological safety. Studies reveal that "the number one factor behind a team's capacity to create value was the presence of what they dubbed 'psychological safety'." This is a workplace condition in which one feels: a) included, b) safe to learn, c) safe to contribute, and d) safe to challenge the status quo, without fear of being embarrassed, marginalized or punished in some way.[32] Conscious Leaders evince this Habit #2 within his/her strong Emotional Intelligence and Service Orientation.

---

30 Source: www.ChrisColbert.com and "7 Habits of Highly Transformative Leaders", Chris Colbert, HU Press (2020).
31 IBID. p.4
32 IBID, p4.

Noteworthy also is Habit #5 whereby transformative leaders create a learning mandate. A shift from Fixed Mindset into Growth Mindset is crucial for anyone to embrace the speed of change occurring in all aspects of modern Life. The primary difference is—an acceptance of failure as temporary and a necessary condition for problem-solving, for advancement. Fixed Mindset abhors failing, believes failure is stigmatizing and a sign of human weakness- hence to be avoided! However, as Chris Colbert emphasizes: "54% of all employees will need significant re-skilling by 2024" and "by 2030, analysts expect automation to eliminate 29% of jobs, while contributing only 13% to job creation."[33]

Digital transformation everywhere evident in healthcare, economy, politics, social media, advertisements and space travel is less about <u>technology</u> than about <u>people</u>. Innovation depends upon people skills. Adoption of innovation requires education and adaptation of people to new ways of doing, having and owning. Willingness to learn is a crucial prerequisite.

A transformative leader shows Habit #5 when "getting every employee to understand that teaching and learning is part of their job, and an essential function of a sustainable future"[34] for the business enterprise. Conscious Leaders practice daily a Growth Mindset and deliberately foster an environment of learning and experimentation.

While there is no accepted single description of key attributes to traditional Excellent Leaders, this listing arises from a general consensus:

1. Self-confidence / will
2. Drive – Passion
3. Persuader – enabler
4. Communicator
5. Courage- boldness
6. Credibility – respected
7. Knowledge – wisdom
8. Committed to Excel
9. Visionary – planner, strategic

The above description presents a normative image of a great Leader – one that is relative to time/place/culture and connected to social norms. In addition, the lynch-pin reference point of Excellent Leadership is productivity in business: an exploitation of inputs to production for maximation of returns—to labor, to material, to time and to capital.

Similar characteristics persist in Exceptional Leaders who also embrace manners and Faith-based, or Spiritual, principles. Here the emphasis is on high moral values, collective good as an end goal and starts with a premise of stewardship and/or trusteeship by man

---

33 IBID p.11
34 IBID. p12

of Earthy resources required for production. Notice that this next listing of attributes can be viewed from the Follower perspective as well as Leader viewpoint.

1. Conviction   Yaqin
2. Risk-taking, drive   Iqdam
3. Sincerity – speaking truth   Iklas
4. Eloquence – clarity of message   Fasahah
5. Excellence in Performance, Manners   Imtiyaz, aladab
6. Humbleness & Patience, Compassion   Sabr, Rahman
7. Knowledge – wisdom in learning, listening   Ilm, Hikmah
8. Unity, brotherhood, equality and Common Good   Takaful
9. God-Conscious – visionary, service, Spiritual   Taqwa

These are attributes of effective Leaders that derive from Arabic terminology/language used in the 7th CE on the Arabian peninsula yet appear to be relevant to Conscious Leaders in 21st CE. By contrast, at that time the reference points for Exceptional Leadership included Stewardship (#8), optimization of existing resources for "the greatest good for the greatest number of people across the community and planet" and Faith (#9).

Colbert's 7 Habits of Transformational Leaders begins to break-free from a traditional understanding of the 20th CE behaviors fundamental to successful business leaders. However, there are some missing elements to a full transition into Conscious Leadership. The following table highlights these.

Table #3. Chris Colbert's 7 Habits in Comparison

Colbert's 7 Habits Transformation Leaders	Traditional Leader Traits	Dr Omar's Conscious Leaders	Comments
Embrace behavior change	Credibility, Committed to Excel	Excellence – behavior (manners) plus biz performance	Shift: mostly financial KPIs (SH value) to humane working, social impact, conscious capitalism
Make psychological safety	Communicator, Persuader	Honesty- sincerity, compassion, safety to challenge	Shift: overcoming objections to buy-in; participatory
Bold intentions	Self-confidence, will, courage, drive	Eloquence/ Conviction – clarity, strategic, credibility	

One plan	Visionary- strategic, Top-down	Unity – consensus, integration of dynamic organization	Shift: matrix/lateral orgz. Structure; diversity of opinions yet One Plan
Learning mandate	Knowledge, Experience (past)	Knowledge – learning, listening wisdom (future)	Shift: past/what works; future/ innovation, experimentation
Biz= customer centric/ outside-in	Profitability, SH growth	Common Good, stakeholders, community alignment	Shift: broader performance KPIs; sustainability, LT Growth
Circle Seekers - talent	Human Capital as producers	Risk-taking – change makers	Talent- stakeholders as partners
		God-Consciousness – Spiritual dimension, service, Leader as Servant (Vulnerability); humbleness, patience	New element: personal fulfillment, impact on 7th Gen

As transition progresses from **Age of Information** into the 21st CE **Age of Conscious**, there are possibly five (5) missing elements in accurate and complete profile of effective 21st CE leadership.

In addition to Traditional Leadership traits, a Conscious Leader must show:

- Self-Knowing Leadership Mindset (deeper level of authenticity)
- Service Orientation (self-Awareness and self-confidence in a "servant role", creating a safe space)
- Growth Mindset (vs. Fixed Mindset and avoid demanding to be always right; operating within a learning mandate)
- Unity of Vision with Sustainability (optimization not maximization, environmental harmony and long-term goals)
- Striving for Conscious Capitalism[35] (vs. short-term profits, efficiency and cut-throat competition)

These additional elements elevate a Traditional Leader to become a Conscious Leader- one who knows themselves, knows clearly their purpose and is both confident and caring in shaping their followers into future leaders.

---

35 Described in Part 10, following.

In short, hallmarks of a powerful Conscious Leader are: Collaboration, Conviction, Personal Clarity and motivating a Community into Collective and Constructive Actions which produce impact.

How to Assess if You are Stuck in Traditional Leadership

According to Kelly Campbell, a professional Conscious Leadership Coach in USA, there are 6 signals[36] a business leader might be stuck in habits consistent with traditional forms of leadership. The headlines adapted from her blog are:

- **Constantly Seeking Approval**
  When you find yourself fishing for compliments after every task or win, there may some deep-seated emotional issues to explore and resolve in order to become a more secure leader.
- **Working Harder with No Obvious Gain**
  No matter how many hours you work, your earnings remain the same or dip. You feel persistent dissatisfaction which causes frustration, self-doubt and a realization that something has to change.
- **Low or Negative Profits**
  Sometimes, there are external factors that deal you a bad blow. Whenever you find that your business profit margin is low, at breakeven or running consistently in the red, it could well be an indication that leadership is inadequate to the situation and needs challenge at the core.
- **More Talking and Less Listening**
  When you talk more than you listen, you can't understand or address issues properly, which means that they tend to arise over and over again. Conscious leaders don't listen to respond, they listen actively and intently in order to understand. Then, they collaborate with others to resolve challenges.
- **Little to No Input From Your Team**
  When your team is silent in meetings. Or when asked for ideas, feedback, etc., they are reluctant to respond, or act half-heartedly. They feel that their opinions will be either dismissed or don't seem to matter to you as the leader. Absent a safe space for their voices to be heard, resentment can build — which eventually leads to internal friction and/or high turn-over and attrition.
- **Weak Accountability**
  When you as leader no longer seem relatable to others. You no longer take full responsibility for decisions and results. If you feel as though you need to have all the answers all the time, you might be alienating those around you.
  Whenever you make a mistake (because you will), you refuse to acknowledge it, avoid being vulnerable and taking responsibility; this often leads to reinforcing a habit of wanting always to be "right". This creates a spiral into isolation and non-accountability, which causes leadership to erode and to weaken overall.

---

36 Section adapted from Dr. Kelly Campbell's "6 Signals that indicate You may be Stuck", internet blog www.klcampbell.com.

Q1. Chris Colbert identifies how many highly transformative habits of Leaders- name at least 4?

Q2. According to the author of this ebook, how many habits are "missing" from behaviors of good Leaders that are necessary for Conscious Leadership? Identify them.

Q3. There are 6 signs that your leadership (or your boss') is stuck in a traditional model. What are these? How to evolve into more transformative habits?

It is apparent that teaching others about financial and operational KPIs is necessary but no longer sufficient- that external performance (market share, ROE/ROI, brand reputation likes) is incomplete for business enterprise today. In order to propel mankind forward through the turmoil of 21st CE rapid change, it is imperative now to teach others mindfulness, self-knowing, service orientation to community and caring to preserve our planet <u>plus</u> achieving sustainable profits.

Conscious Leadership is a new way of thinking and being in the workplace. The next section describes the qualities of Conscious Leaders.

Part 8. Qualities of a Conscious Leader

So what is Conscious Leadership?

Conscious Leadership in business refers to **guiding others with full awareness of the self and cultivating growth in organizations by supporting the people in them**. Instead of focus revolving around an ego-centric 'ME first" attitude, a Conscious Leader is "self-knowing" and embodies an inclusive 'WE first" approach.[37]

Why is "Conscious" important in the new style of Leadership?

Conscious Leadership responds to prevailing rapid changes and challenges of 21st CE by **consistently leading a transformation of one's personal worldview, personal relationships, and company culture guided by constructive and sustainable long-term goals**. Apart from nurturing growth in their professional career context, Conscious Leaders also flourish in their personal lives, and their charisma inspires and empowers those around them to do the same.

---

37 Source:https://www.sunderlandcoaching.com/blog/what-is-conscious-leadership-a-quick-guide

Those leaders who are not yet practicing Conscious Leadership, may be said to be "Unconscious leaders". As Farrar-Eagles, explains:

> "An Unconscious Leader is one who **makes decisions completely unaware of how their decision or behavior is going to impact others.**"

Their personal focus is on "ME", on self-interest, on "getting ahead" in a fiercely competitive business environment of winners and losers. Short-term (often quarterly) objectives – largely framed as financial results – dominate thinking and are reinforced by corporate incentives, rewards and recognitions.

Framework for becoming a Conscious Leader (more in Part 7. and Part 9 following)

There are 4 pillars that shape a strong foundation for being a Conscious Leader.

> - **Self-Leadership** – becoming a Conscious Leader (CEO of my Life); taking 100% responsibility, compassionate, self-directed [transit out of victim mentality, feeling being "stuck" and/or sense of entitlement
> - **Integrity** – live/speak my truth; being authentic
> - **Holistic Development** – develop 4 Realms of Growth[38] into harmony & balance
> - **Sufficiency & Sustainability** – for yourself <u>and</u> the Planet [to transit away from: consumerism mentality; more is always better; debt and credit leverage vs. assets; money ignorance to money mastery]

These are End Goals that act as guiding lights in the mind of a Conscious Leader.

The 4 Realms of Growth to be harmonized by the individual are:

a. Mind – Intellect
b. Heart – Emotions
c. Cellular – Self-Identity
d. Spirit – Purpose-driven Life; acknowledging Unity of all things

For more, reference **Part 5.** and **Part 11.** herein.

What are the Specific Qualities/Behaviors of Conscious Leaders

Conscious Leaders abundantly display many of the qualities we most admire in exemplary human beings. They usually find great joy and beauty in their work, and in the opportunity to serve, lead, and help shape a better future. Since they are living their calling, they are authentic individuals who are eager to share their passion with others. They are very dedicated to their work, which recharges and energizes them instead of draining them.

---

38 Refer to Part 5. And pp. 41-45.

Conscious Leaders commonly have high analytical, emotional, spiritual, and systems intelligence. They also have an orientation toward servant leadership, high integrity, and a great capacity for love and caring.

There is no one-size-fits-all model of leadership. Conscious Leaders have much in common with each other, but much more that is unique to each individual as they advance on their personal journey of self-discovery.

They are keenly self-aware and recognize their own deepest motivations and convictions. They don't try to be someone they are not. As Bill George, former CEO of Medtronic, puts it, "Great leadership is authentic leadership. Authenticity is not a characteristic; it is **who** you are. It means knowing who you are and what your purpose is. Your True North is what you believe at the deepest level, what truly defines you—your beliefs, your values, your passions, and the principles you live by."[39]

Authenticity is a consequence of natural integration and harmonization of four (4) behavioral dimensions: IQ, EQ, SQ and SYQ.

Diagram #7.

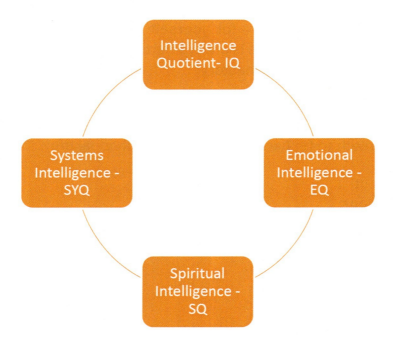

Let's examine each.[40]

Intelligence Quotient - IQ

Most conscious leaders have high analytical intelligence (the kind measured by IQ and similar psychological tests). This is a prerequisite for being a successful leader today in

39 **Authentic Leadership - Bill George,** https://www.billgeorge.org
40 Adapted from John Mackey, Conscious Capitalism, USA 2014

large, complex business organizations. Problem-solving and oversight of corporation transformation requires a blend of IQ and imagination. But having a high IQ without also having high Emotional Intelligence (EQ), Spiritual Intelligence (SQ), and Systems Intelligence (SYQ) is inadequate and may be harmful to an organization. Bad decisions will be made based on short-term considerations that lack a system wide perspective of what is good for all of the interdependent stakeholders over the long-term and ignores impacts on the sustainability of Mother Earth.

Emotional Intelligence

EQ combines intrapersonal (understanding oneself) and interpersonal (understanding others) intelligence. Self-awareness, the core of what it means to be more conscious, is the first pillar of emotional intelligence. Empathy—the ability to feel and understand what others are feeling—is the second pillar. High EQ is increasingly important in all organizations because of the growing complexity of society and the multiplicity of stakeholders that must be understood and communicated with effectively. An over-emphasis of EQ can cause poor analysis of organizational or systems needs. Likewise, EQ must be guided by moral values and clarity on the purpose of the business.

Spiritual Intelligence

Conscious Leaders frequently have high SQ, which has been well defined in a wonderful book by Danah Zohar and Ian Marshall titled Spiritual Capital:

> "Spiritual intelligence is the intelligence with which we access our deepest meanings, values, purposes, and higher motivations. It is ... our moral intelligence, giving us an innate ability to distinguish right from wrong. It is the intelligence with which we exercise goodness, truth, beauty, and compassion in our lives."[41]

SQ is what helps to discover a personal higher purposes in our work and our lives. Conscious Leaders with high SQ have a remarkable ability to communicate widely and help to align their employees and their organization with their organizations' higher purposes. People seek to bond with others and to a higher calling that accumulates individual "Spiritual (Psychic) Capital" [*author's term*] and delivers a collective sense of mission and purpose daily.

Systems Intelligence

Conscious Leaders are natural systems thinkers. They exhibit strong SYQ when they see the bigger picture and understand how the different components of the system interconnect and behave over time for benefit of their organization. They can anticipate the immediate as well as long-term consequences of management decisions and

---

41 Danah Zohar and Ian Marshall, Spiritual Capital, https://danahzohar.com/books/capital, UK, 2004

actions. Given their intuitive understanding of systems, Conscious Leaders are excellent organizational architects. They understand the roots of problems and how the problems relate to organizational design, and hence they can devise fundamental solutions instead of applying symptomatic quick fixes.

Conscious Leaders are also systems feelers: they feel the interconnectedness and oneness of the system within their being.[42] As a result, they can prevent many problems from occurring in the first place.

Conscious Leaders, with their strong analytical, emotional, spiritual, and system intelligences, are acutely aware of the importance of **service to all stakeholders** in helping their organizations realize their highest potential. Attention to service/contribution both inside and outside the business, leads others to experience more personal satisfaction and work-related happiness.

Such leaders have learned the secret of the "helpers' high:" we feel good when we make other people happy. It creates value for the giver and the recipient, as well as for the larger community. Servant leaders cultivate the noble virtue of generosity. They embrace transpersonal values—such as goodness, justice, truth, love, the alleviation of suffering, the salvation or enlightenment of others—that lift them to higher levels of consciousness.

One challenge here is to do this while emanating "unconditional Love" [500 and above on Dawkins scale, p.72], giving without judgment from a solid place of self-knowing, neutrality as to outcomes and aiming at the best good for others in the situation.

The story of Buckminster Fuller provides a great illustration of the power of servant leadership. What would make life worth living? In a sudden flash of spiritual insight, the answer came to him. He would begin "an experiment, to determine how much a single individual could contribute to changing the world and benefiting all humankind."[43] The answer, it turns out, is "quite a lot." Over the next fifty-five years until his death, he patented over two thousand inventions, wrote twenty-five books, and went down in history as one of the greatest thinkers, inventors, and servant leaders who ever lived. The Buckminster Fuller game of doing as much good as possible to benefit the world is a game we can all play. Servant leaders show us how to do this.

To summarize the characteristics and attitudes of Conscious Leaders, here is a convenient (but not exhaustive) checklist:

Table #4. Conscious Leader Attributes—10 to Thrive

- o Organizer – takes action, makes decision, direct, plans
- o Is Authority – 100% responsible, controlling (empathy), credible, Will, delegates

---

42 John Mackey, Conscious Capitalism, USA 2014
43 John Rajendra, Forward to Mackey's Conscious Capitalism, USA, 2014

- o Displays Intelligence – visionary, passion & purpose, strategic, sees Big Picture (imagination & **IQ intelligence**)
- o Resourceful – mobilize needed resources, problem-solving (**Systems intelligence**), innovate, resilient, risk taking
- o Motivator – develops others, incentives and rewards/acknowledgement
- o Communicator – clarity of messages, persuasion, courage (from conviction)
- o Compassionate—**Emotional intelligence**, empathy, heart-centered,
- o Authentic – true to self, self-belief, honest, speaks truth, intuitive
- o Spiritual – self-aware, aware of higher-self (**Spiritual intelligence**), ethical thinking and behaviors, attention to 7th generation- long term impacts, examines consequences
- o Possesses Mastery – nurtures Will/execution, deploys applied skills-Experience, Wisdom (listens over speaks), sustains Balance, continuous learning

Two points stand out as absent from traditional business Leaders and central to the concept of Conscious Leaders; namely:

- A Conscious Leader is a role model of manners and "good" behaviors
- A Conscious Leader is Authentic and Self-aware- meaning aspiring to equally know him/her-self and their Higher Self (Spiritual dimension)

Generally, across modern corporate business environments these two topics are avoided. Ideas emerged in the 1960s-1970s, were labelled as "touchy-feely" and "fuzzy" features not viewed as central to successful business C-suite leaders. Also, the re-birth of such ideas described five (5) decades later as "emotional intelligence" and/or "leader as servant" are circulating certainly yet over-shadowed still by relentless measurement of quarter-to-quarter profits, revenue growth, shareholder earnings and expansion of pricing power across corporate networks.

The boundary line between Traditional Leadership and Conscious Leadership is visible when comparing these two attributes—quite pointedly visible using a lens of ESG's whereby Traditional Leaders are mostly unconvinced their corporations influence climate change adversely, need to examine and measure their carbon footprint, sustainability and environmental impact: simply, their leadership as reflected in corporate culture and manners is impeccable "as is". Of course, there exist a few company role model exceptions. Examples are: CIMB Bank in Malaysia; Square hi-tech in USA and Body Shop retail consumer in USA.

How does this theory play out in the rough and tumble business world today- we explore next what Conscious Leaders do.

What Conscious Leaders Do

Conscious Leaders seek to make a positive impact on the world through their organization. They deeply embed a sense of shared purpose, enabling people to derive meaning from their work. They help people grow and evolve as individuals and, eventually, to grow into leaders in their own right, and they make tough moral choices with clarity and consistency. Conscious Leaders are natural role models for "Service to Others", living out the Servant Style of Leadership.

Conscious Leaders believe there is "good" in everything, choose to seek out that "good" (however small a part) and harness positive energies of business community (both inside and outside) toward shared higher ideals. They display persistence and determination, but do not pander to ego or self-gratification. Rather than seeking to be right always—to prove their title, superiority or to impose their will on the business organization-- Conscious Leaders are aligned to their sense of compassion and empathy so as to serve the collective spirit and organizational vision.

Why does Conscious Leadership matter?

For millennia, most men (and they were mostly men) who became leaders were driven to attain these roles because of their thirst for power or lust for riches. They used fear, oppression, and brutality to achieve their goals. But their successes were inevitably short-lived, because the leaders' actions continually sowed the seeds of the next upheaval, the next rebellion, the emergence of the next ruthless and self-serving leader.

The possibility of Conscious Leadership matters today more than ever. Old ways of Traditional Leadership are obsolete and have run its cycle. Leadership in the third millennium must be based on the power of Self-knowing, purpose, love, caring, and compassion. Conscious Leadership is fully human leadership- neither overly male nor overly female. Instead, it integrates the masculine and feminine power [here reference Dr. Hawkins' POWER vs FORCE excerpt in Appendix **A3**], the heart and the mind, the spirit and the soul. It integrates Western philosophy of pragmatic systems blended with efficiency and Eastern philosophy of wisdom blended with effectiveness.

Drawing on decades of consulting and studies with major international corporations, Jim Dethmer, Diana Chapman and Kaley W. Klemp, published a detailed examination of behaviors of Conscious Leaders in corporate contexts. Their book (2014) is entitled: *The 15 Commitments of Conscious Leadership*." Therein, Conscious Leadership is defined as "the process by which a leader becomes radically responsible, self-aware, and focuses on building a culture of "we" rather than a culture of "me."

Significant findings and examples presented in the book on what Conscious Leaders DO may be set forth here:

- A Conscious Leader is emotionally and spiritually mature. Possesses high self-esteem, is motivated to nurture and lead others, displays moral courage, curiosity, openness, a willing to learn. Applies a Growth Mindset.
- A Conscious Leader is driven by the purpose of the Business. Is mindful of developing benefits to stakeholders (not just shareholders/stock price/IPO), rather

than personal enrichment, and acts as trustee of business assets, safeguards its organizational dynamism and special resources for future generations (rather than quarterly profits).

- A Conscious Leader is a mentor, who inspires, develops followers (to become leaders) to strive to achieve their own potential and acts as role model. Famously, Mahatma Gandhi once said: "We must be the change we wish to see in the world." Also, Quranic verse translation of Ar Rad V13:11 says: "Lo! God changeth not the condition of a folk until they (first) change that which is in their hearts.."

Leadership is NOT the same as Management. **Leadership** is all about transformation, change, shaping behaviors in business across an organization (dynamic, people oriented, affecting the mosaic of community). **Management** is about efficiency, effectiveness, systems, processes, decisions and implementation of plans.

What is needed most today in business is harmony between the **L** and **M**. As Harvard Business School Professor John Kotter puts it, "Too much **management** without enough leadership leads to too much stability and inward focus. This eventually results in stagnation, decline and probably the death of the organization. Too much **leadership** without enough management is also dangerous; the company lacks organizational capacity, operational discipline and efficiency, and the business can become very risky."[44] Very concisely Kotter stated: "Leadership is about coping with change; whereas management is about coping with complexity." And again: "Management is focused on creating order through processes, whereas leadership is focused on creating change through vision."

INSERT EXERCISE 6. – Key Quality Questions to help focus a journey to becoming a Conscious Leader.

Q1. What are the 4 elements of a Conscious Leader? Are these equally important-influential?

Q2. Describe the 4 Pillars of an eco-system that supports Conscious Leadership in action?

Q3. Conscious Leaders are recognized for display of 10 attributes. Name/describe as many as you can.

Q4. Clearly explain the difference between "Management" and "Leadership".

Q5. In your own words, describe what Conscious Leadership matters and what can this contribute to mankind in the coming three decades.

---

44 Professor John Kotter, Leadership vs Management, writings at HBS 1987.

So how does a leader evolve into a Conscious Leader? Answers to this pivotal question come in the next section.

Part 9. Becoming a Conscious Leader

As discussed previously, the mindset and operational framework to be adopted by a Conscious Leader includes:

- Growth Mindset and shaping a holistic approach to Self-development
- Being Authentic, truthful and credible
- Practicing Curiosity through continuous learning, testing & failing
- Refocus is P3 – Profits, People, Planet, with decisions looking into 7th Generation timeline
- Advancing Conscious Capitalism, assuring WIN for All (as opposed to WIN-LOSE), orienting Cause above Self and seeking Common Ground and the Common Good

This framework draws careful attention to the Mental and Emotional behaviors of the Leader. Nothing less than Mastery of the 4 Realms of Growth, styles of human behavior, is required (Part 8). No one Mindset remains permanently fixed—the Conscious Leader responds to changing practical business circumstances, yet aspires to practice Style# 4 (Spiritual Achievement) as consistently as possible.

Diagram #8. Mindsets

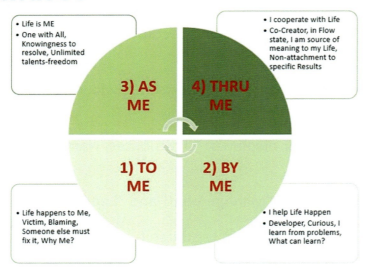
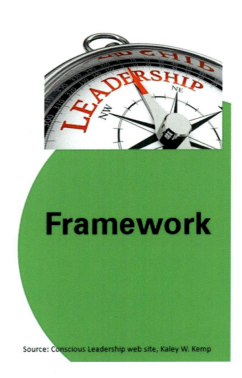

Source: Conscious Leadership web site, Kaley W. Kemp

With specific reference to leader mindset, the goal of Conscious Leadership is Mastery of these 4 Mindsets (States of Affair) so as to completely master **Self-Leadership** first. It is difficult to lead others before <u>first</u> learning to lead oneself. Also, only then is a Conscious

Leader properly equipped to lead others --- across the full spectrum of various relations: family, friends, business, healthcare, politics, etc. As consistently as possible, a Conscious Leader operates with the 4th Mindset- "Thru Me."

How to Progress into Conscious Leadership

When stepping away from the application of leadership into corporate working environments and back into realm of the individual, the central focal point returns to Mindset. Inevitably, the Conscious Leader strives for harmonization of his/her Inside and Outside realities. This is realized when balancing four (4) levels of human Awareness. [refer to previous Diagram #8.]

Consciousness flows into and throughout the human body and mind in the 3rd and 4th Dimensions, which cannot exist separate nor apart from an integrated and whole fabric of Time/Space. Each person experiences Conscious as integral, unified and covalent yet at any moment in Time that individual's attention may be giving more importance to (responding to) a single dimension (more 3rd D or 4th D); i.e. Body and rush of feelings or Spiritual yearnings and internal stillness.

How Conscious Leadership Informs Dynamic Organizational Success

Business success is leading collaborative teams of people who are fulfilled because they are valued in every way and are empowered to put customers' interests first. This formula breeds success because it leads to higher productivity, more effective and satisfactory work, and results in client retention plus new business, all in combination generates more revenues and higher profit margins.[45]

How do Conscious Leaders help their organizations to succeed[46]:

1. **Higher Levels of Self-Awareness**
   When a leader knows themselves well, that knowledge helps them to regulate their emotions and be more intentional in their behavior and actions in different circumstances, which results in positive interactions and outcomes with team members, partners, clients, and prospects.

2. **Level-Headedness**
   A calm and sensible leader is trusted more than one who is impulsive and explosive. Conflict is sure to arise in business and when it does, a conscious leader approaches the situation in a way that allows people to feel heard and secure (leaders create "psychic safety").

---

45 Refer back to **Part 1**. P.6 – potential for 10X returns.
46 Adapted from Blog by Kelly Campbell, USA Author, www.consciousnessleaders.com

3. **Intentional**

   When you're intentional you have a purpose behind every activity. For the conscious leader, the intention is communicated so that it also works to set an example for others to bring more intention to their own interactions and work.

4. **Constant Self-Improvement**

   More knowledge means more expertise and ultimately a better future. In this case, it often leads you to seek <u>coaching</u> in the arena of mindset, shadow work, and overall leadership development for the benefit of your team, yourself and the organization as a whole.

5. **Compassionate**

   Compassion and empathy are key character traits for Conscious Leaders. It adorns the way they speak, address challenges, and encourage others to improve. With time, this sets the precedent and becomes ingrained the company's **Conscious Culture** itself.

When you see Conscious Leaders in action- what evidence might we witness?

- A Leader who is emotionally and spiritually mature (EQ & SQ), having high self-esteem, motivated to nurture and lead others, displaying moral courage, curiosity, open minded and willing to learn (Growth Mindset)
- A Leader who is driven by purpose of the business, amassing benefits to stakeholders (not just shareholders/stock price/IPO), and rather than seeking personal enrichment, acts as a trustee of that business, safeguards its organization/resources for future generations (rather than quarterly profits) and concentrates on balancing corporate profits with social impacts
- A Leader who is inspiring, a mentor that develops followers (to become leaders) and acts as role model. Recall the quote by Mahatma Gandhi "We must be the change we wish to see in the world."

  Take note: we repeat that Leadership is <u>not</u> the same as Management. **Leadership** is about transformation, change, shaping human behaviors in a commercial business across an organization (dynamic, people oriented, mosaic community). Whereas **Management** is about efficiency, effectiveness, systems, processes, implementation and outcomes.

Managers do not make change that gets recorded into history; Conscious Leaders do. They imagine and bring into existence that which did not exist before, which most people thought could not be done, and they co-create this new reality with followers.

Personal transformation into a Conscious Leader can be confirmed visibly from the resultant changes in behavior and attitude towards business and stakeholders, yet mostly the necessary changes are actually internal to that leader. Moreover, these changes cannot happen overnight-- rather the human transformation is more akin to morphic change: 1 +

1 = 3. Holistic inner modifications collaborate and synergistically generate a new, more expansive outcome. Similar in nature to evolution state changes that transmogrify the butterfly:

Diagram #9. Butterfly Stages

Stages   Egg or Larva

          Voracious Caterpillar

          Sleepy Pupa or Cocoon

          Full Hatching of an adult Butterfly

The end result—Butterfly – is innate to the Egg yet requires a total transformation, a shedding of prior "identity" and attributes to make room for a complete metamorphosis.

Steps to Become a Conscious Leader

A typical natural life cycle of a butterfly is 3 to 6 months. Few overnight changes in the natural world of Time/Space are enduring. Therefore, evolution into a Conscious Leader is expected to pass through stages (including unlearning and re-learning behaviors) that might extend 6 to 12 months, or longer.

Diagram #10. Steps to Adoption

Typical 6 Steps to Adoption

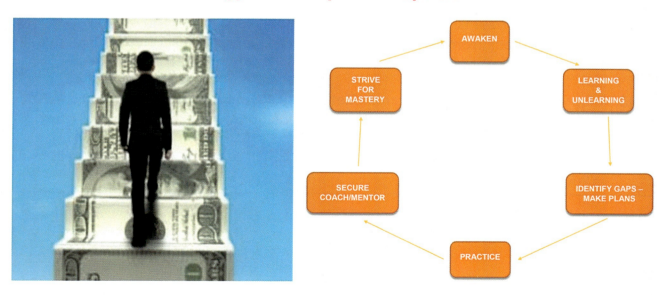

Process of adoption into Conscious Leadership can be teased out a bit into 6 main Steps to Self-Mastery:

- Awakening –
- Learning and Unlearning – framework basics
- Identify Gaps – where to build Bridges / develop a Plan & set new goals
- Practice Daily – establish morning routine, establish feedback loops, reconcile failures
- Obtain Mentor – seeking coaching, accountability to help shed old habits
- Strive for Mastery – accelerated learning, maturation into a Conscious Leader, Self-Mastery as authentic, purposeful, expert

---

Metaphor of Butterfly

1. Egg: Sleeping to Awakening; learning & unlearning
2. Caterpillar: Identify Gaps – develop plan set goals, build bridges
3. Pupa: Obtain Coach, Mentor – daily practice, shed old habits/ skin & mistakes, refine
4. Butterfly: Self-Mastery – try new learnings (wings), accelerated learning, gain experience, independence, validation, result is beautiful to behold…

What the rapid change of the 21st CE demands of business leaders is to evolve into Conscious Leaders. Make no mistake: Conscious Leaders are responsible to lead the organization into profitability. Without profits, no business enterprise can survive. However, Conscious Leaders also commit to Conscious Capitalism- the topic we cover next.

INSERT EXERCISE 7. – Key Quality Questions to help focus a journey to becoming a Conscious Leader.

Q1. There are 5 points of focus for becoming a Conscious Leaders. What are these?

Q2. A Growth Mindset is crucial for personal evolution. Explain the 4 quadrants and how to progress from one to another. Which quadrant describes your mindset-most of the time?

Q3. Adoption of Conscious Leader mindset may occur in 6 steps. What are they? Which step most closely aligns with your current position?

Q4. In what ways can a Conscious Leader impact her/his company and propel it forward?

Part 10. Leading into Conscious Capitalism

"Excellence is not a gift, but a skill that takes practice. We do not act 'rightly' because we are 'excellent', in fact we achieve 'excellence' by acting 'rightly.'"

-- Plato 4th BCE

What are the 4 main types of economic systems?

There are four types of economies:

- Pure Market Economy– **Capitalism**
- Pure Command Economy – Communism
- Agrarian Economy
- Socialist Economy- Socialism, mixture of State-owned enterprises making profits for private/state shareholders

The most important aspects of a capitalist system are **private property, private control of the factors of production, accumulation of capital, and competition**. Put simply, a capitalist system is controlled by market forces, while a communist system is controlled by and serves national government objectives.

What is the basic goal of capitalism?

Capitalism is an economic system in which private actors own and control property in accord with their self interests, and demand and supply freely set prices in markets in a way that can serve the best interests of consumers and generate highest marginal profits for shareholders. The essential feature of capitalism is **the motive to make a profit through efficient utilization of the factors of production**.

Capitalism is a version of national economic system that perpetuates power and influence to providers of capital over labor and material factors of production. Capitalist economies operate on the basis of **private property, supply and demand, marketplace competition, freedom of pricing and incentives to individual performance**. Also, Capitalism when compared to alternative national economic systems of socialism or communism, has unique features such as **private ownership of property and means of production, a financial profit motive, minimal government intervention, competition** and has demonstrated a natural evolution from agrarian to industrial to knowledge-based business enterprises.

The basic goal of Capitalism is maximization of profit motive. This generally causes tight control of expenses (including labor costs), maximizing efficiencies and margins, and aligning incentives and rewards to revenue (and earnings) growth more than stakeholder personal growth or preserving the long-term sustainability of its environment and the planet. Financial best interests of shareholders are superior objectives to broader (and often non-financial) interests of stakeholders and society.

Diagram #11. Tenets of Conscious Capitalism[47]

The four tenets of Conscious Capitalism

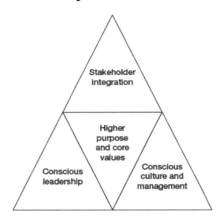

What is Conscious Capitalism and how does it differ from Capitalism?

Firstly, Capitalism is gradually evolving and making room to include corporate social responsibility (CSR); however, Conscious Capitalism goes even further on because it perceives society and common interests of social communities to be a chief stakeholder in the business itself. Hence, a business operations must be socially responsible from its outset. Moreover, a conscious business steers towards higher purposes (that serve society's greater good), gives attention to stakeholders over shareholders and transcends the hallmark of service-oriented leadership. So what more is called upon?

While adhering to the constructive aspects of Capitalism, Conscious Capitalism expands a Leader's perspective to encompass:

- Conscious Self-Leadership
- Embracing a higher Purpose for the business (the anchor reference point rather than maximization of profits solely)
- Diligently nurturing Conscious Leadership traits in followers and employees-eventually evolving into a **Conscious Culture** for the business enterprise itself

Let's recall Drucker's famous maxim: "Culture eats Strategy for breakfast every time in business."

Therefore, to excel in a transformative commercial setting prevailing in the 21st CE, leaders must learn how become Conscious Leaders and inculcate these prime three (3) aspects into and throughout their organizations: Higher Purpose, Conscious Leadership Inside and Outside (supply chain) and a Conscious Culture.

John Mackey, CEO and founder of Whole Foods (USA retailer) is credited with having invented the term "Conscious Capitalism" in the 1980s. Soon afterwards, he co-authored

---

47 Source: John Mackey's book <u>Conscious Capitalism</u>, 2014.

a book with that title combining the marketing expertise of Raj Sisodia. In 2009, Raj and Shubhro Sen founded the Conscious Capitalism Institute to perform research and development plus spread the Conscious Capitalism teachings globally. Conscious Capitalism is more than simply good business and espousing platitudes as ideals.

There are four pillars to **Conscious Capitalism.**

The four guiding principles behind conscious capitalism include **a higher purpose, stakeholder orientation, conscious leadership, and conscious culture.**

When integrated in corporate decisions and actions, these guiding principles elevate a business above social responsibility- actually, interact so as to modify the core beliefs driving a business, its dynamic systems and processes, and uplifts its personnel in partnership with stakeholders to strive for more than outstanding financial results and market share.

On a more practical note, Conscious Capitalism differs from Capitalism in its preoccupation with <u>Co-existence and Sustainability</u> – often decisions assess and reflect long-term impacts on the coming 7th generation![48]

<u>Co-Existence</u> recognizes reciprocity between people and planet; keeping in mind that nearly all material factors of production derive from Earthly resources.

Professor Rajendra Sisodia, from Bentley University, succinctly describes Conscious Capitalism in his viewpoint article (2014)[49]. He refers to an early synopsis that equates an individual leader's conscious with that of his business:

> "To be conscious means to be awake, mindful. To live consciously means to be open to perceiving the world around and within us, to understand our circumstances, and to decide how to respond to them in ways that honor our needs, values, and goals [...] A conscious business fosters peace and happiness in the individual, respect and solidarity in the community, and mission accomplishment in the organization (Fred Kofman, 2006)." [50]

---

48 Native American Indian guiding principle.
49 Professor Rajendra Sisodia, "Doing Business in the age of conscious capitalism", originally published in Journal of Indian Business Research, found on www.researchgate.net/publication/235252046
50 Cited from a book by Fred Kohman, <u>How to Build Value through Values</u>, p.3, 2006.

Although Conscious Capitalism accepts Competition and open market-exchanges, it avoids the fierce cut-throat Competition and mentality of "Conquest" of Natural resources because these lead to exploitation, depletion and eventual exhaustion of resources. For example: new genetically engineered seeds require fertilizers which require more water, leave residue on plants and introduce toxicity into our Food Chain. Yes, tonnage of rice/wheat is temporarily higher….yet fertile ground get "exhausted".

Capitalism posits a strong maximization strategy – more is always better; while this generates increased profits, the maximization strategy often destroys cooperation, erodes sustainability, conflicts with a mentality looking long-term, and crowds out optimization strategies favoring Sustainability.

> "Capitalism, done consciously, is the most powerful system for uplifting humankind to unimaginable levels of prosperity, peace, and happiness. [Mackey's] book identifies the forces of light and makes an impassioned plea for them.

> "Conscious Capitalism is in keeping with the ancient wisdom of India as it views leadership as trusteeship: focusing on the right actions and not being unduly attached to outcome." —The Economic Times /2016

Conscious Capitalism embraces a Conscious Culture across the company—"leadership as trusteeship" as stated above.

As stated earlier, the four guiding principles behind Conscious Capitalism are: **a higher purpose, stakeholder orientation, conscious leadership, and conscious culture**.

Hence, harnessing the proven system of Capitalism, if done consciously, is an extremely powerful economic system for uplifting humankind to higher levels of prosperity, peace, and happiness. This EBook seeks to identify the attributes of a new breed of leaders for the 21st CE, describes the process for inculcation and makes an impassioned plea for their rapid and wide adoption.

What is a Conscious Culture?

Looking inwards to business operations, cultivating a **Conscious Culture** is absolutely necessary for steerage towards and, eventual realization of, Conscious Capitalism. Among the prominent qualities of **Conscious Culture** are:

- Accountability
- Integrity
- Trust
- Transparency
- Fairness
- Mutual Respect and sense of employee Safety

While these qualities may seem esoteric or abstract/subjective, fortunately, there are some role models of corporations which today practice **Conscious Capitalism**.

Here are some examples of CEOs in USA who practice Conscious Culture even when confronted with extraordinary and devastating economic challenges:

"47 CEOs Taking Pay Cuts To Help Their Companies Survive the Coronavirus: *Executives across a number of industries are cutting their pay.*"[51]

Certainly a CEO paycut, even a substantial one, is not prerequisite for Conscious Leadership, nor alone does it confirm it. Rather, these are extraordinary measures/decisions taken willingly by company heads in order to: i) reduce operating expenses, ii) shift the burden of a necessary payroll reduction from workers to management, thus preserving the incomes of employees (and avoiding layoffs), iii) demonstrating sacrifice as a leader to underpin survival of the company, and iv) signal that hard times can be shared by stakeholders as one team. Collectively, signs of Conscious Leadership. Examples are:

- Guess Co. CEO Carlos Alberini, cut base salary of $1.2 M by 70%
- REI Co, CEO Eric Artz, cut base salary of $850,000 by 100%
- Wyndham Hotels, CEO Geoff Ballotti, cut base salary of $888,191 by 100%
- VOX Media, CEO Jim Bankoff, cut base salary by 50%
- Columbia Sportwear Co., CEO Tim Boyle cut base salary of $950,532 to just $10,000
- Walt Disney Co., CEO Bob Chapek cut base salary of $2.5 M by 50%

A **Conscious Culture** is one in which both management and employees practice self-awareness of the environment they're part of and one where everyone feels accountable, empowered, and expected to act in a way that is in accordance with the corporate values (culture) that the company seeks to foster-- consistent with its stated brand and presence in the marketplace.

Which companies practice Conscious Capitalism?

A number of recognizable brands demonstrate the principles of Conscious Capitalism, including: **Whole Foods Market, Starbucks, Trader Joe's, The Body Shop, Ben and Jerry's, Patagonia, COSTCO. Southwest Airlines** is another example, with its focus on a triple bottom line approach that attributes equal value to people, planet, and profits (known as the 3P's).

---

51 To Start a Business Blog, article by Gabrielle Olya, Nov 2020.

An increasing number of globally recognizable brands demonstrate the principles of conscious capitalism, including **Whole Foods Market, Google, Starbucks, Trader Joe's, and The Container Store**.

Part 11. Benefits of Conscious Leaders and the 5th Dimension

Benefits of Conscious Leadership affect the Leader in two (2) aspects:

- Benefits Inside the Leader – self-confidence, empathy, effectiveness in leading and upgrade in self-awareness and sense of well-being
- Benefits Outside the Leader – across business organization, impact in its marketplace, stimulating and inspiring stakeholders and the community of followers, and ideally a lasting impact on society

Specifically,

Inside affects involve the revitalization of individual conscious and consistent mindfulness in human Leaders. Over and above the business acumen, authenticity and credibility traits displayed are a level of self-mastery and disciplined self-awareness which blend as an impressive role model to inspire others. A chief focus of Conscious Leaders is guiding stakeholders towards their own self-fulfillment by tapping into their productive energies and potential.

Outside affects revolve around innovation, resourceful problem-solving in the business context so as to refresh sustainability and corporate leadership. Business KPIs are expanded to address preservation of environment, seeking substitution into renewable energies, drawing upon "tribal diversity" rather then homogenization of opinions, stimulating imagination and innovation (vs. limited incremental changes), and advancement of Conscious Capitalism and means-goals over old-fashioned capitalistic end-goals.

In addition, on a national scale **Outside** affects promote a sharing economy, collaboration rather then pure competition, and the redirection of national resources away from military and weapons to reduce human poverty, hunger, and improve elderly healthcare, universal medical care, early childhood education and research into probing depths of Conscious and other knowledge advancements.

Moreover when accelerating human conscious development, going beyond 3rd-4th Dimensions, this requires projecting our innate creativity and imagination into the 5th Dimension. 4th Dimension Time awareness contains familiar yet unseen components of Time/Space, but is studied with instruments available to mankind that measure in terms of Time/Space – such as distance, molecules or atoms which negates purity of experience and defies measurement.

5th Dimension is unseen and wholly unknowable, yet exists most likely relative to other recognizable dimensions. Clues appear to reside within hyperspace, Black and White Holes occurring naturally in outer space, resultant of the organizing Intelligence that permeates all Universes. 5th Dimension encompasses the Collective Conscious and is linked to Cosmic Conscious as a child is linked to a parent. Since 5th Dimension emanates spirituality, although is not its origin, language is obviously inadequate to capture its essential nature, or portray how it functions. Thus, human conscious evolution into the 5th Dimension is much more of a promise than a certainty.

On The Way to 5th Dimension Conscious

By extrapolation, human conscious transformation into and acceptance of the 5th Dimension requires seeking harmonization and re-balancing among 4 Realms of Growth which are levels of Human Awareness.

1. **Mind** – intellectual; knowledge yet does not do; comfort zone; 90% habitual behaviors; more than biochemistry of Brain…extends by magnetic field some 3 meters beyond Body; 2 parts: conscious/logic/analytical AND subconscious-habits, patterns, instinct, memories/images
2. **Body** – physical field governed by human brain and 17 types of Emotions (Energy in Motion); coherent feelings with Mind support or conflicted, stress, dis-ease; makes memories vital infused with "feelings" / hence can be storehouse for hurt, injury, trauma/ sometimes 'Hidden" from Mind; includes Heart (2nd Mind)
3. **Soul** – Self-Identity; individual accountability; co-creator; moments in Time/Space progressing- guided by Beliefs (stored in Subconscious Mind); blend of ancient DNA inherited Beliefs and accretion of new Understandings- present day; engaged with personal Will
4. **Spirit**- Divine Spark – the eternal, Infinite All Knowing Intelligence flowing through all Creation; accretion of all Knowledge, Data, Wisdom, Purpose; Timeless; embodied into each human before birth and engaged during Lifetime, always linked to Cosmic Will.

These 4 Realms of Growth-- Levels of Awareness are profiled in the following Table #4.

Table #4. Harmonization of 4 Levels of Human Awareness

	4 Levels of Awareness	Dimension	Description	Comments
Intellect	Mind	3rd Dimension of Brain/Heart plus a 4th Dimension— awareness of Time & Space	Intellectual; knowledge yet does not do; comfort zone; 90% habitual behaviors; more than biochemistry of Brain… extends by magnetic field some 3 meters beyond Body	Brain & vibrations/ aura Start of awareness of Consciousness
Emotional	Body	3rd Dimension – length, height, width & vibration (affecting 4th D)	physical field; 17 types of Emotions = Energy in Motion; coherent feelings with Mind support or conflicted, stress, dis-ease; moody; individual feelings – understanding at GUT level;	Self-Awareness-control on Emotions; Heart-felt; Sex-Love
Cellular	Soul	5th Dimension-4D + hyperspace	Self-Identity; individual accountability; co-creator; Imagination	DNA data; Core Beliefs; concept of SpaceTime 91 Bil Light Yrs.; Pure Love
Spiritual	Spirit	+6th Dimension – field of all possibilities	Eternal, Infinite All Knowing Intelligence flowing through all Creation; accretion of all Knowledge, Data, Wisdom, Purpose	Transcendence; Collective Consciousness; Unconditional Love

In the event that a Conscious Leader successfully achieves harmonization, it is postulated that there can be some participation within the 5th Dimension, which exists as an extra dimension of hyperspace relative to Time/Space. Such a dimension was proposed independently by physicists Oskar Klein and Theodor Kaluza in the 1920s. They were inspired by **Einstein's theory of gravity**, which showed that mass warps four-dimensional space-time.[52]

They speculated that one starting point for the 5th Dimension is a mysterious connection between the universal Law of Gravity and electromagnetic wave-force. One analogy is swimming underwater when a drop hits just below the surface of ocean causing ripples and sound vibrations. Or a mother's love (and light) towards an inconsolable crying baby bolstered by Source Energy of Unconditional Love flowing through the "ocean of pure Love" intermingled with the Collective Conscious extant outside the 4th Dimension of Time/Space.

---

52 VH Satheeshkumar, article on Laws of Gravity, www.arvix.org/ pdf 2006.

Q1. Briefly describe the benefits of Conscious Leadership to the individual and to the company or business environment.

Q2. If there were a 5th Dimension to Life, how could it be described?

Q3. There are at least 4 Realms for Human Growth- explain each.

Q4. A Conscious Leader harmonizes these 4 Realms, which produces what outcomes?

Q5. If one percent (1%) of humanity evolved into Conscious Leaders and tapped the 5th Dimension, what is the likely result for human evolution and for our planet Earth?

Part 12. Conclusions

In short, this EBook is an urgent Call to Action. Mankind must take seriously a necessity to move beyond the mindset of the 20th CE and reach for its enormous (and unchartered) potential and unlimited range of possibilities accessible through an evolution of human **Conscious**-ness. Such life-changing transformation needs leaders. Traditional Leadership styles and role models are outdated and inadequate to such advancement.

It all begins with Self-awareness and commitment to Self-growth. Some advice to readers who are excited to take up this challenge:

❖ Self-growth is more than possible, it is now imperative and most likely experienced as exponential rather than linear growth

❖ Stop waiting – just do it

❖ Stop seeking exoneration – validation of always being "right", instead embrace adventure and be ready to explore

❖ Stop excusing yourself because you are not yet "perfect"; failures and mistakes mean learning is happening; focus on the journey itself not the destination; struggles in Life are inevitable, so don't wait for these to end first

❖ Stop Learned Helplessness – waiting on someone else to solve your troubles; instead improve self-confidence and self-reliance

❖ Realize Self-improvement requires Self-Healing – start here, forgiveness of Self and Others who may have caused hurt; take each fresh new day as bringing new opportunities; release the past, heal the hurts, and embrace the present as a gift with gratitude.

- Get Self-Awareness switched ON! No longer "sleep-walking" [Unconscious]
- Paradigm in your Mind controls your thinking/decisions/behaviors (i.e. **Performance**) and ultimately **RESULTS**
- Not simply about GETTING….about Doing, Having, and ultimately Be-coming
- Collaboration – Cooperation vanquishes all challenges
- Recall Tony Robbins said: "Life is all about WHO you want to BECOME."
- Capitalism (like a gun) is not itself BAD, it is how it is used.

Avoid the traditional WIN-LOSE capitalist competitive mindset. Replace this. Strive consciously for WIN-WIN attitude towards employees, stakeholders, with clients, with partners.

"Why as we age, do we spend more time in preparing to Die than Living? Surely Living Well and fully Being is its own best preparation for non-Living." - Carl Jung

For more information on how to become a Conscious Leader, visit www.consciouswealth. me, or email omar@consciouswealth.me, or arrange a phone call (free) at https:// calendly.com/omar-fisher/letstalk .

~~ End
resources/links

======================= /

14. Appendices

Appendix A1. Author's Journey to Conscious

My personal journey into Conscious began as a boy growing up in Waban, a suburb of Newton some 11 miles outside Boston, Mass. At my parents' insistence, I attended bible school on Sundays in the basement of our Episcopal Church. Fascinated with the trappings of that church—the hard wood benches, stained glass windows, the lit candles on the alter and the ornate flowing habits of the Minister, so I volunteered to assist him as Alter Boy during communions.

Moreover, I read the King James version (1948) in English of the Holy Bible multiple times. Stories therein captivated my imagination, offered wise lessons but listings of generations of lineage of leaders and prophets bemuse and bewilder me to this date.

At age 18, I drove a yellow 1967 mustang convertible from Chicago, IL to San Francisco, CA as an adventure in independence. My trusty steel-bodied Nikon camera captured in remarkable Ektachrome color the wonders of American nature, national parks, rivers and wilderness as I drove west.

My first conscious experience unfolded among the majestic redwood trees in Muir Woods.[53] My curiosity with spiritual methods prompted me while studying at university to explore the Sufi House in New Haven and to participate in several lectures and retreats on weekends. One standout retreat was to home of Mohamed Muhieddine, a Sufi Master, who passed some time in outskirts of Philadelphia. Also, I pursued instruction in Transcendental Meditation ("TM") as promulgated by Maharishi Mahesh Yogi, which evolved into a twice daily practice of quiet meditation.

Living in Cambridge, MA close by Harvard University permitted me to imbibe unlimited poetry from the Lamont Poetry Library and the renown Grolier Poetry Bookstore (original owner Gordon Carnie allowed me to borrow books overnight provided I promised not to soil the paper covers). Moreover, I participated in an all-male workshop led by Laurie Handlers for "Opening the Heart", out of which grew a male support group to practice active listening, meditation and becoming attuned to feelings.

The next summer, I rode a motorcycle throughout 8 countries in Europe—from UK, France, Switzerland, Italy, Austria, Czech Republic, Germany, and Holland—keen to witness cathedrals, churches, houses of worship, art galleries and stunning natural vistas.

My attraction to Eastern philosophy deepened with readings of <u>Bhagavad-Gita As It Is</u> (A.C. B. Swami Prabhupada), <u>The Secret Doctrine</u> (Vol.1, H.P. Blavatsky), <u>The Tao of Abundance</u> (Laurence G. Boldt) and <u>Change Your Thoughts-Change Your Life</u> (Dr. Wayne Dyer), and I expanded my inquiry into eastern national economic systems- with focus on China. During 1976-78, I actively participated in the U.S.-China Friendship Association of Boston, which resulted in my selection among the first 52 Americans to visit China since 1948-- to embark on a 3-week study tour of PRC in summer 1978.

This was fortuitous as a few months prior, I was accepted into the Arthur D. Little International Business School (Cambridge, MA and forerunner to HULT International Business School which merged in 2009). This intensive Science of Management program was taught by AD Little expert practitioners with curriculum concentrated on international business practices in emerging markets.

On my return leg from China, I arranged to travel into Thailand and India. The ancient capital of Ayutthaya (Empire of Siam in 1350/14 CE) featured astounding Buddhists temples some more than 2 thousand years old. My sojourn in India took me from Mumbai to an ashram in ancient city of Poona, where I listened to evenings lectures of Bhagwan Rajneesh Osho Ji (1978). Nearby, I visited and meditated in the Ajanta and Ellora caves near Aurangabad where amazing 35ft deep caves were carved by monks in 2nd BCE (to 5th CE) into hard rock on the 400 foot sheer face of a cliff accessible only by rope ladders.

---

53 I eventually made a return visit to these redwoods in 2018, 50+ years later, which inspired my poem "Listening to the Redwoods".

Here again, I deliberately sought out temples, churches, houses of worship and places of quiet prayer. At each sacred spot, I meditated for some time absorbing the ancient vibrations and enhancing my spiritual practice.

ADL assigned me to Cairo, Egypt (1980-82) as a residential management consultant on a telephony transformation project. Truly inspirational experiences enthralled me upon visiting the Giza Pyramids, the even older Saqqara Mastabas', and the Luxor painted temples and burial sites of Upper Egypt.

Between 1983-1992, I was very fortunate to travel extensively for my work as an Investment Guarantee Officer at the Overseas Private Investment Corporation ("OPIC") from Washington, D.C. into the Caribbean Islands, and Middle East-North Africa, visiting more than 26 countries.

Again, I carried my daily meditation practice into these foreign and exotic places. While living in Cairo, there was opportunity to witness Islamic character first-hand and to question the religious tenets of Islam. I discovered that my beloved stories in the Bible were repeated with detail in the Quran (revelation sent to Prophet Muhammed in 7th CE) and certain unreconciled questions were resolved to me. As a Christian in childhood, I learned about and respected all the declared prophets sent as messengers to mankind.

When I embraced Islam in 1980 at Al Azar University (Cairo), my spiritual journey ascended with recognition of the unity in all and everything. Further, my Conscious expanded bolstered by casual readings and webinars about quantum field physics—being mentored by Dr. Joe DiSpenza, Deepak Chopra, Bob Proctor, Napoleon Hill, Marc Fisher, James Allen, Nassim Haramein, Vishin Lakhani, Tony Robbins, to name a few.

A career move to Jeddah, Saudi Arabia in 2000 further opened my mind to spiritual practice and provided me once-in-a-lifetime experiences of worship at the centuries old sacred temples in Makkah and Madinah. Performance of Hajj (2001 and 2003) and visits to Cave of Hira and battlegrounds of Badr and Ahzab (or Battle of the Trenches) outside Madinah, accentuated my self-awareness of core beliefs, being authentic and submission to a Life Purpose of service and contribution using my God-given unique talents. Nothing in the ensuing 20 years journey of self-discovery dissuades me from these essential truths.

On the contrary, the authorship in 2020 of Conscious Wealth and in 2022 of this EBook on Conscious Leadership are consistent endeavors to illuminate the journey of Spirituality and Conscious-ness that is available to everyone – each in their own way and timing.

There are 19 gates to Heaven, each guarded by an angel. I pray that my personal Spiritual path outlined here may be instructive of the possibilities open to you, dear Reader.

> "Ask, and it shall be given you; seek, and ye. shall find; knock, and it shall be opened unto you: / For every one that asketh receiveth; and he that seeketh. Findeth…" Matthew 7:7-8 KJV

Seek within for Conscious- the pure I AM.

"...for the Kingdom of Heaven is within". Luke 17:21.

"...to Gabriel - for he brings down the (revelation) to thy heart by Allah's will, a confirmation of what went before, and guidance and glad tidings for those who believe..." Quran V2:97 Al Baqarah:The Cow

===================== /

Appendix A2. Fundamental Realizations: Occurring at Beginning of The Way to Self-Actualization

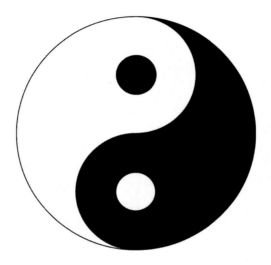

"I AM" when spoken in self-talk consists of 2 elements: "I" and "AM". Understanding can be facilitated by reflecting upon the ancient symbol of Yin and Yang (shown above).

"I AM" is an individual SOUL speaking to itself. The "YOU" doing the speaking is seemingly a second person speaking to "ME". Or restated as the Cosmic Conscious "I" speaking to the individual "AM", temporarily imprisoned in Time/Space. "AM" experiences itself as ME, in the first person, the unique Body/Mind co-existing in this present moment. AM is having a Self-awareness of this Body/Mind known through sensations, feelings and a perception of NOW in Time. This Self-awareness is Conscious. Hence, Conscious is flowing into and through that individual Soul as AM.

The "I" originates from Cosmic Conscious being it emanates from the Prime Mover (as a Divine Spark), the Totality of All, the singular Creator of All there Is, which is an All-Knowing Intelligence flowing into and by Conscious with unfathomable Order and Purpose.

Typically, we experience this "YOU" speaking [self-talk- inner thoughts] as "external" to ME. Yet in fact, both the "I" and "AM" are co-existent, co-dependent and mutually

reinforcing (like YANG-YIN concept). Only in entering Pure Consciousness does "AM" feel fully complete and integrated (transcendent) with "I".

Daily, each of us lives in Time & Space (4 Dimensions) and within degrees of personal mindfulness. We may enrich our conscious to experience more deeply the 4th D, and possibly the 5th Dimension [by mental elevation beyond Time/Space described as Nirvana or Bliss state]. Most people choose to live in 3rd D and understand I AM as other than themselves – a YOU speaking occasionally with ME.

A refined, enlightened Conscious AM may catch pulses/glimpses of vibrant Pure Energy as Conscious, which is ever-present equally in all directions and all levels; meaning a 6th Dimension of the Prime "I" – invisible, All-knowing, Unity of Intelligence, Source Energy, pure Spirituality, yet incomprehensible to human ken locked within limits imposed by Time/Space.

Appendix A3. Dr. David Hawkins' Map of Consciousness (2012)

THE MAP OF CONSCIOUSNESS – HAWKINS' SCALE[54]

Introduction

On our journey throughout life we find ourselves met by all kinds of people and all kinds of situations and experiences. Our ability to learn and grow from these experiences is based largely on our ability to discern truth from falsehood. It has been demonstrated over the eons that the human mind is incapable of discerning truth as the stunning evidence of pain and suffering mounts, not only at the individual level but also at the level of entire civilizations. Dr. David R. Hawkins, MD, PhD has created a tool that he calls the Map of Consciousness. This map was developed to overcome the inherent limitation of the human mind, whereby falsity has been misidentified as truth. His ultimate goal "is a connecting of the dots so that the hidden picture emerges. The hope is that this work might undo the very sources of pain, suffering, and failure, and assist the evolution of human consciousness in each of us to rise to the level of joy that should be the essence of each and every human being's experience".

Background

The Map of Consciousness was created by Dr. David Hawkins, a psychiatrist, who experienced several life-altering events throughout his life. Following each event, he noticed a change in his state of consciousness from an ego-based/ mind focus to a completely overwhelming state of overpowering bliss where he felt a constant, steady connection with the "Presence".

---

54 Excerpts from paper published By Carla M. Thompson, RN, BscN; January 19, 2012 (Copyright 2012), ref. www.stankovuniversallaw.com

With this dramatic change in his level of consciousness, he decided that he must pursue the reason why it had changed and how he could describe the changes to help mankind in the pursuit of enlightenment. His driving desire was to "address the causes of the endless stream of spiritual distress and human suffering".

History

The Map of Consciousness is a numerical scale whereby one can measure positive from negative, power from force and truth from falsehood. Dr. Hawkins believes that every word, every thought, and every intention creates what is called a morphogenetic field[55], or attractor field, and that these energy fields can be measured by a very simple process. This process is a well-established science known as Kinesiology. Kinesiology is defined as the study of muscles and their movements, especially as applied to physical conditioning. The study of kinesiology first gained scientific attention from the work of Dr. George Goodheart, who pioneered the specialty he called Applied Kinesiology, after finding that benign physical stimuli such as beneficial vitamin and mineral supplements would increase the strength of certain indicator muscles, whereas hostile stimuli would cause those muscles to suddenly weaken.

In the late 1970s, Dr. John Diamond refined this specialty into Behavioral Kinesiology where indicator muscles would strengthen or weaken in the presence of positive or negative physical, emotional and intellectual stimuli.

God-View	Self-View	Level	Log Scale	Emotion	Process
Self-Consciousness	Is	Enlightenment	700-1,000	Ineffable	Pure Conscious
All-Being	Perfect	Peace	600	Bliss	Illumination
Oneness	Complete	Joy	540	Serenity	Transfiguration
Loving	Benign	Love	500	Reverence	Revelation
Wise	Meaningful	Reason	400	Understanding	Abstraction
Merciful	Harmonious	Acceptance	350	Forgiveness	Transcendence

---

55 Explanation of morphogentic field: "Rupert Sheldrake talks about morphogenetic fields (or M-fields) as invisible organizing patterns that act like energy templates to establish forms on various levels of life, eg: when Sir Roger Bannister broke the 4-minute mile, he created a new M-field.
"Natural systems, or morphic units, at all levels of complexity — atoms, molecules, crystals, cells, tissues, organs, organisms, and societies of organisms — are animated, organized, and coordinated by morphic fields, which contain an inherent memory. Natural systems inherit this collective memory from all previous things of their kind by a process called morphic resonance, with the result that patterns of development and behavior become increasingly habitual through repetition. There is a continuous spectrum of morphic fields, including morphogenetic fields, behavioral fields, mental fields, and social and cultural fields." ~ Rubert Sheldrake. Source: https://elis-med.com

Inspiring	Hopeful	Willingness	310	Optimism	Intention
Enabling	Satisfactory	Neutrality	250	Trust	Release
Permitting	Feasible	Courage	200	Affirmation	Empowerment
Source:	Dr. David Hawkins				

Dr. Hawkins' research took Dr. Diamond's technique several steps further, by discovering that this kinesiologic response conveys man's capacity to differentiate not only positive from negative stimuli, but also anabolic from catabolic, and very dramatically, truth from falsity. The Map of Consciousness reflects millions of calibrations of statements, thoughts, photos, art, music, influential world leaders in every discipline and in almost every area of human endeavor. The research carried on for over 20 years to come up effectively with an anatomy of consciousness that reflects the entire human condition.

Table #5. Dr. Hawkins' MAP OF THE SCALE OF CONSCIOUSNESS

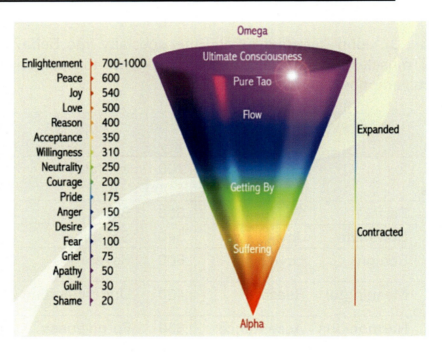

Source: https://www.smritiagrawal.com/maslow

Table #6. LEVELS OF TRUTH/ LEVELS OF FALSEHOOD

God-View	Self-View	Level	Log Scale	Emotion	Process
Indifferent	Demanding	Pride	175	Scorn	Inflation
Vengeful	Antagonistic	Anger	150	Hate	Aggression
Denying	Disappointing	Desire	125	Craving	Enslavement
Punitive	Frightening	Fear	100	Anxiety	Withdrawal
Uncaring	Tragic	Grief	75	Regret	Despondency
Condemning	Hopeless	Apathy, Hatred	50	Despair	Abdication
Vindictive	Evil	Guilt	30	Blame	Destruction
Despising	Hateful	Shame	20	Humiliation	Elimination
Source:	Dr. David Hawkins				

Application

Consciousness has no limits in space or time. The answers to questions posed do not depend upon the belief systems of either the tester or the test subject. Consciousness knows only truth because only truth exists in reality. It does not respond to falsehood because falsehood has no existence in reality. It will not respond to non-integrity questions nor those that are ego-based. A good example of this type of questioning would include asking which Stock to buy, and so on.

The critical point between positive and negative, between true and false, or between constructive and destructive is at the calibrated level of 200.

In his book Healing and Recovery (2009), Dr. Hawkins illustrates the effects of levels of consciousness on society. This can inform us today of relative importance of teaching youth and adults alike presence of mind, self-love and broader impacts of personal behaviors:

Table #7. Consciousness and Societal Problems

Correlation of Levels of Consciousness and Societal Problems

Level of Consciousness	Rate of Unemployment	Poverty	Rate of Happiness "Life is OK"	Rate Criminality
600+	0%	0.0%	100%	0.0%
500-600	0%	0.0%	98%	0.5%
400-500	2%	0.5%	70%	2.0%
300-400	7%	1.0%	50%	5.0%
200-300	8%	1.5%	40%	9.0%
100-200	50%	22.0%	15%	50.0%
50-100	75%	40.0%	2%	91.0%
<50	97%	65.0%	0%	98.0%

Source: Through Cindy S. Yantis (2017)....

Notice that this scale is a logarithmic progression. Therefore, the level of 300 is not twice the amplitude of 150; it is 10 to the 300th power. An increase of even a few points is indicative of a major advance in power.

Levels Below 200

The lower levels of consciousness include Shame, Guilt/Hate, Apathy, Grief, Fear, Desire, Anger and Pride. These levels are the most painful that we experience and it is the pain that these levels create that drive us in our desire for understanding and inner growth. Perhaps it is not our full intention to grow, spiritually, but this becomes the result after much inner reflection and discussion. These levels are dominated by falsehood.

Dr. Hawkins describes these lower levels of consciousness as **ego** dominated life where one thrives on the techniques and emotions of animal survival. These are aligned with pleasure, predation and gain. Below the 200 level, an individual is left-brain dominant (in right-handed people), which means that input goes directly to the amygdala (almond), so emotional response is triggered before intelligence and cognition. From this orientation, others are seen as objects or means to personal survival.

Calibration levels 200 – 500 Linear Mind

In human consciousness, there is a huge transition at the level of 200 where right brain dominance (in right-handed people) reflects the increasing influence of spiritual energy and a reliance now on Power rather than Force. At this point, input is fast-tracked directly to the pre-frontal cortex and the emotional center. This influence brings progressive awareness and openness to the energy of love. These levels include Courage, Neutrality, Willingness, Acceptance, and Reason. These levels also increasingly align with truth.

The level 500-599 is a defining level of love where it is not just a feeling but a principle to live one's life by. Only 4 percent of the worlds population reaches the level of '500' and only 0.4 percent reach level '540'.

Dr. Hawkins has created charts which engage the reader in considering alternate possibilities to awareness. By simply reading these charts one is shown a point of view from the "other side". The effect is in increasing awareness of one's own positions and how some character "defects" will actually subside as soon as they are recognized and owned.

Table #8. Functions of Mind – Attitudes A

Lower Mind (cal. 155)	Higher Mind (cal. 275)
Accumulation	Growth
Acquire	Savor
Remember	Reflect
Maintain	Evolve
Think	Process
Denotation	Inference
Time = restriction	Time = opportunity
Focus on present/past	Focus on present/future
Ruled by emotions/wants	Ruled by reason/inspiration
Blames	Takes responsibility
Careless	Disciplined
Content (Specifics)	Content plus field (conditions)
Concrete, literal	Abstract, imaginative
Limited, time, space	Unlimited
Personal	Impersonal
Form	Significance
Focus on specifics	Generalities
Exclusive examples	Categorize class – inclusive
Reactive	Detached

Passive/aggressive	Protective
Recall events	Contextualize significance
Plan	Create
Definition	Essence, meaningful
Particularize	Generalize
Pedestrian	Transcendent
Motivation	Inspirational, intention
Morals	Ethics
Examples	Principles
Physical and Emotional survival	Intellectual development
Pleasure and satisfaction	Fulfillment of potential

Table #9. Functions of Mind – Attitudes B

Lower Mind (cal. 155)	Higher Mind (cal. 275)
Impatient	Tolerant
Demand	Prefer
Desire	Value
Upset, tension	Calm, deliberate
Control	Let go, surrender
Utilitarian use	Sees potential
Literal	Intuitive
Ego-self directed	Ego, plus other-oriented
Personal & family survival	Survival of others
Constrictive	Expansive
Exploit, use up	Preserve, enhance
Design	Art
Competition	Cooperation
Pretty, attractive	Aesthetics
Naive, impressionable	Sophisticated, informed
Guilt	Regret
Gullible	Thoughtful
Pessimist	Optimist
Excess	Balance
Force	**Power**
Smart, clever	Intelligent
Exploits life	Serves life
Callous	Merciful
Insensitive	Sensitive

Particularize	Contextualize
Statement	Hypothesis
Closure	Open-ended
Terminal	Germinal
Sympathize	Empathize
Rate	Evaluate
Want	Choose
Avoid	Face and Accept
Childish	Mature
Attacks	Avoids
Critical	Accepting
Condemning	Forgiving
Skepticism	Comprehend

Congratulations! Your level of consciousness has risen as you have read this article. As new ideas push the <u>morphogenetic</u> field outward, new attractor fields are built, breaking through old thought forms and beliefs driven by force and new belief systems are created. As more of us think about this topic and these considerations, larger and larger fields are created. As we share this information with others, we are in turn creating ever larger <u>M-fields</u>, breaking the bonds of Force and Falsehood and engaging Power and Truth. You have surely assisted in the learning process by increasing your level of consciousness and therefore the advancement of Humanity.

This moment in our evolution is one that requires discernment as we effectively identify issues that represent Truth and those that are heavy with deception. We are awakening to the truth that the failures of our institutions are a result of the implementation of FORCE and as we have learned from this research, anything that is based on force, is disconnected from Source. Humanity has grown accustomed to the illusion of isolation and separation. Dr. Hawkins has proven through the power in kinesiology, that there is a connection between the two universes, the physical and the mind and spirit. He states "in a world full of sleepers lost from their source, here was a tool to recover that lost connection with the higher reality and demonstrate it for all to see". We are all connected to the Source.

In Conclusion:

Remember, The Map of Consciousness test takes a lot of practice to create a reliable result. Ultimately, a number value itself is not as important as being able to discern Power over Force (sometimes easier to see than Truth over Falsehood). In time, you will recognize how these ideas "feel" to you. You will find yourself using a combination of how you might "feel" about something, and combine it with what you intuit about a situation. As you begin to trust in your own inner knowing, you will be able eventually to discern truth from falsehood very quickly and easily. You will finally master the Art of Discernment. For this is the year of TRUTH.

Enslavement by illusion is comfortable;
it is the liberation by Truth that people fear.
Straight and narrow is the path…
Waste no time.
Gloria in Excelsis Deo!
Dr. David R. Hawkins

BIBLIOGRAPHY	REFERENCES	
Book Title	Author	Publisher
The happiness track: Apply the science of happiness to accelerate your success	Emma Seppala, PhD	HarperOne, 2016
The Science of Happiness-how our brains make us happy	Stefan Klein, PhD	Scribe, 2015
The Millionaire Next Door	Thomas Stanley, William Danko	Pocket Books, Simon & Schuster, 1996
Power vs. Force	Dr. David R. Hawkins	Hay House, New York, 2002
You2	Price Pritchett, PhD	PP, Dallas, TX, 2016
Creating Affluence	Deepak Chopra	New World Library, CA,1992
The Seven Spiritual Laws of Success	Deepak Chopra	New World Library, New York, 1994
The Success Principles	Jack Canfield	HarperElement, 2005
The Science of Success	Wallace D. Wattles	Fall river Press, 2017, originals 1910
The Soul of Money- transform your relationship with money and life	Lynne Twist	WW Norton & Co, NY 2017
The Observer (11 January 1931); also.	Erwin Schrodinger	in Psychic Research (1931), Vol. 25, p. 91
"Do We Have a Soul? And What is the Conscious Universe?"	James Lynn	Blog 3rd February 2017
"The Mental Universe"	R.C. Henry	NATURE, Vol. 436, July 2005. P17
Acres of Diamonds	Jentezen Franklin	Chosen- Baker Publishing Group. MN 2020
8 Pillars of Prosperity & Other Writings	James Allen	Wilco Books, Mumbai India, 2011 original 1901

Ancient Puzzle: Connection of Money & Happiness	Omar Fisher, PhD	Self-Published, 2018 Grasshopper Series EBook
15 Things You Should Give Up to be Happy	Luminita D. Saviue	Perigee Books, Penguin, 2016 NY
Reflections on Happiness & Positivity	Mohammed bin Rashid Al Maktoum	Explorer Publishing, Executive Office, Dubai 2017
The Science of getting Rich	Wallace D. Wattles, forward by Bob Proctor	Proctor Gallagher Institute, AZ 2014 reprint
Financial Freedom: Proven Path to All the Money You Will Ever Need	Grant Sabatier	Penguin Random House, NY 2020
The 21 Irrefutable Laws of Leadership	John C. Maxwell	Thomas Nelson Publishers, TN 1998
You're Going to Need a Bigger Wallet: Hands On Financial literacy	Nick Erskine	CreatesSpace, 2017 TX
The Deficit Myth: Modern Monetary Theory	Stephanie Kelton	John Murray Publishers, UK 2020
Your Money Made Simple: Key to Financial Freedom	Russ Crosson	Harvest House Publishers, OR USA 1995
I Can Make You Rich	Paul McKenna	Transworld Publishers, London, UK 2008
A Millionaire's Notebook: How Ordinary People can achieve Extraordinary Success	Steven K. Scott	Fireside Book, Simon & Schuster, NY 1996
Change Your Life in 7 Days	Paul McKenna	Bantam Press, Transworld Publishers, London, UK 2004
Dollars and Sense: How we misthink Money	Dan Arieley and Jeff Kreisler	Harper Collins, NY 2017
Wealth Attraction in the New Economy	Dan S. Kennedy	Eliot House Productions, Canada, 2010
GET REAL! The Real Secret of Success Revealed	Innocent A. Izamoje	Top Consulting Ltd, Cox & Wyman Printers, 2002 UK
How Will You Measure Your Life?	Clayton M. Christensen	HarperCollins Publishers, New York, 2012
The 7 Habits of Highly Effective People	Stephen R. Covey	Fireside Books, Simon & Schuster, NY 1990

The Answer	John Assaraf and Murray Smith	Simon & Schuster, NY 2008
Automatic Wealth- 6 steps to Financial Independence	Michael Masterson	John Wiley & Sons, New Jersey, 2005
The Truth About Money	Ric Edelman	Harper Business, H.Collins Publishers, New York 1996
Creating Money- Attracting Abundance	Sanaya Roman & Duane Packer	New World Library, Calif, 2008
Financial Planning Essentials	Ernst & Young	John Wiley & Sons, 1999
Conscious Wealth: 30 day blueprint to Financial Freedom	Dr. Omar Fisher	Passionpreneur Publishers, Dubai/ Sydney, AU Ingram Press, 2022
The Official Guide to Success	Tom Hopkins	Warner Books, New York, 1982
How to master the Art of Selling	Tom Hopkins	Warner Books, 1982
Unlimited Power	Anthony Robbins	Fawcett Combine Publishers, New York, 1987
Creating Wealth	Robert G. Allen	Simon & Schuster, New York, 1987
Flight of the Buffalo: Soaring to Excellence	James A. Belasco, and Ralph C. Stayer	Warner Books, New York, 1993
Blue Ocean Strategy	W.Chan Kim, Renee Mauborgne	Harvard University Press, Cambridge, 2005
Competing for the Future	Gary Hamel, C.K. Prahalad	Harvard University Press, Cambridge, 1994

==================

Appendix A Four. Dr. Omar Fisher Author Profile

~~ end

Dr. Omar's journey into self-awareness and becoming conscious began more than 50 years ago. Many teachers, gurus, mentors and sacred places have shaped his spiritual conscious as recounted in an appendix in this book. Alongside this, his extensive career as a serial entrepreneur with 9 startups in financial services located in USA, Saudi Arabia, Bahrain and United Arab Emirates, gave rise to a rich understanding of business leadership tools, techniques and styles.

When fused with a steady daily mindfulness practice over these 50 years, Dr. Omar's personal evolution as a Thinker and Author results in this illuminating book: "Becoming a Conscious Leader: Gateway to the 5th Dimension." One of his favorite sayings is: "You cannot lead others until first you lead yourself."

Dr. Omar is author to numerous articles, book chapters, untold numbers of webinars and video modules including topics: leasing finance, risk management, investment guarantees, mutual insurance (takaful), Islamic project finance, personal wealth building. Recently, two of his books were published on Financial Intelligence and may be purchased through Amazon or his web site: www.omarfisher.com:

Guide to Financial Intelligence- Faith and Money in the 21st CE

(https://www.amazon.com/Cleanwealth-Guide-Financial-Intelligence-Century-ebook/dp/B094XSV29F)

Conscious Wealth: 30 day Blueprint to Financial Freedom (https://www.amazon.com/Conscious-Wealth-Omar-Fisher/dp/1922456748)

Besides being an author, Dr. Omar is an avid ocean sailor, loves tennis, hiking in the woods and swimming nearly every day. His travels to 44 countries across 4 continents are captured in amateur photography that is happily shared amongst friends and his four children.

May this book be a spark that kindles your inspiration to evolve as a Conscious Leader and empowers you to share confidently your talents, gifts and inner light with our troubled world.